WHAT MAKES YOUR TEEN TICK?

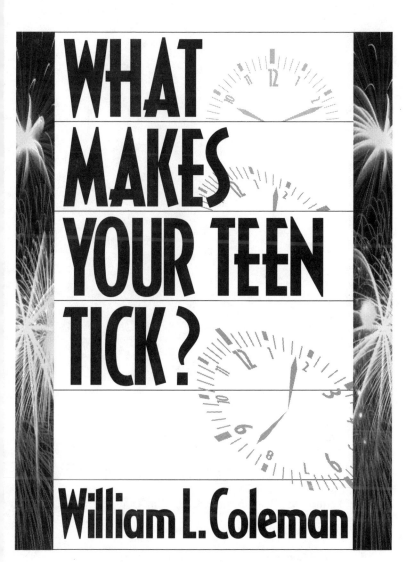

WHAT MAKES YOUR TEEN TICK?

William L. Coleman

BETHANY HOUSE PUBLISHERS
MINNEAPOLIS, MINNESOTA 55438

Published by Bethany House Publishers
A Ministry of Bethany Fellowship, Inc.
6820 Auto Club Road, Minneapolis, Minnesota 55438

Printed in the United States of America

Library of Congress Cataloging-in-Publication Data

Coleman, William L.
    What makes your teen tick /William L. Coleman
        p.   cm.
    1. Parent and teenager
I. Title.
HQ799.15.C66   1993
306.874—dc20   93-18130
ISBN 1–55661–322–9   CIP

A Note From the Author

Freddie and the Supreme Court

When my eldest daughter, Mary, was two years old, she received a huge stuffed dog from her grandfather. Larger than Mary, it became known as Freddie. Freddie wore well over the years, taking many trips with the family, going to summer camp, attending slumber parties, and otherwise living happily in Mary's bedroom.

Twenty-three years later, Mary, then in law school, prepared to present her first case before the Nebraska Supreme Court. As she carefully rehearsed her arguments, Mary placed her favorite childhood dolls, teddy bears, and a beaver on her living room couch to represent the Supreme Court. There in the middle of this distinguished body she placed her old friend, Freddie. For one evening, Freddie became the Chief Justice and listened intently as Mary delivered her most passionate plea.

Freddie and Mary have come a long way together. It was fun watching Mary grow, mature, and meet each of life's challenges. During the process, Mary, like our other children, maneuvered her way through the adolescent years. The teen years in our family, and probably yours as well, have been times of fun, tension, pleasure, and absolute despair.

This book isn't an autobiography. The message isn't: "We have a terrific family; don't you wish you had one, too?" Anyone who knows us would only laugh at that assumption. As one of our grown children said the other day, "Sooner or later we had every authority figure in town call our house for one reason or another." And it's true.

Along the way we learned a few things. We listened to many families and teenagers who told us what they experienced. In the process we read a host of books and found these to be a good way to discover what was normal.

Our goal for this book is that it be practical and realistic, from the humble perspective of survivors. It's a book of hope. Going beyond mere survival, families in the midst of *teendom* can flourish. Parents and teenagers can develop mutual respect, satisfaction, and even pride in one another.

Have you ever seen a young adult with his or her parents actually enjoying the company of each other? Then you have seen life at its richest.

Read, discuss, get involved, and wear a helmet.

Bill and Pat Coleman
December 26, 1992

Books by William Coleman
from Bethany House Publishers

CHESAPEAKE CHARLIE SERIES
  Chesapeake Charlie and the Bay Bank Robbers
  Chesapeake Charlie and Blackbeard's Treasure
  Chesapeake Charlie and the Haunted Ship
  Chesapeake Charlie and the Stolen Diamond

DEVOTIONALS FOR FAMILIES WITH YOUNG CHILDREN
  Animals That Show and Tell
  Before You Tuck Me In
  Getting Ready for Our New Baby
  If Animals Could Talk
  Listen to the Animals
  My Hospital Book
  My Magnificent Machine
  Singing Penguins and Puffed-Up Toads
  Today I Feel Like a Warm Fuzzy
  Today I Feel Shy
  Warm Hug Book

DEVOTIONALS FOR TEENS
  Earning Your Wings
  Friends Forever

It's Been a Good Year
Knit Together
Measured Pace
Newlywed Book
Ten Things Your Teens Will Thank You For . . . Someday
Today's Handbook of Bible Times and Customs
What Children Need to Know When Parents Get Divorced
What Makes Your Teen Tick?

Contents

Introduction: Parenting and Insanity 13

1. The Physical Explosion 19
2. Four Needs Never Change............... 25
3. Developing Teen-Esteem 31
4. Help Your Teenager Cope
   With Frustration 39
5. Ten Conversation Starters................ 45
6. Can You Trust Your Teenager?........... 63
7. Teen Tension 59
8. Moody and Brooding.................... 67
9. Center Stage 71
10. Playing the Rebel 77
11. The Teen's Life Is Different 87
12. How Well Do You Know Your Teen?..... 93
13. What the Teen Needs From Parents 97
14. How to Argue With a Teenager..........107
15. Bribes and Rewards.....................115
16. Kidnapped by Their Peers 121

17. Counseling Your Teenagers 129
18. Trouble With the Truth 135
19. The Need to Believe 139
20. The Need for Forgiveness 147
Conclusion: There Is Reason to Hope! 153

Introduction

Parenting and Insanity

When Jim was sixteen he told us he wanted to bring his date home after they went out. That sounded great to us. Pat and I straightened up the living room, fluffed the pillows on the couch, and waited for the young couple to arrive.

We felt very cool. Two young, vibrant teenagers were choosing to end their date by coming to our house to spend time with some pretty hip parents. We could feel the goose bumps rising on the back of our necks.

Around 10:30, Jim and his date walked through the front door and stopped at the living room entrance. Our son waved his hand toward us and said, "Hi, we're going to watch TV."

Before we could utter a word they hurried down the stairs to the family room in the basement.

So much for us being hip parents. We weren't going to get to rap or groove or whatever it is cool people do.

For a few minutes Pat and I went back to reading *National Geographic* and *Saturday Evening Post,* but we couldn't concentrate. Both of us were thinking the same thing. *What are they doing in the basement?*

Normally, 10:30 is past Pat's bedtime, but on this night she was wide awake. Suddenly she stood up and scurried upstairs, returning a moment later wearing a pair of high-heeled shoes. I simply sat there bewildered, looking at pictures of Romania.

Pat went to the basement door and started carrying things up and down the wooden staircase. CLUNK! CLUNK! CLUNK! Her heels hit the steps like gunshots.

Sticking her head quickly into the family room, she announced, "Popcorn! Anybody want popcorn? I'll fix it."

CLUNK! CLUNK! CLUNK! She was back upstairs in the kitchen popping corn.

Ten minutes later Pat was downstairs again with arms full of soft drinks, napkins, and buttered popcorn. "Just let me know if you want more."

She then collected a basketful of dirty clothes and headed for the basement laundry room. By this time it was past 11:00. SWISH. SWISH. SWISH. Pat topped off her plan by throwing a pair of tennis shoes into the dryer. KABOOM. KABOOM. KABOOM. They sounded like a bass drum.

Once she had all of the domestic chores underway, she darted her smiling face back into the family room.

"Brownies?" she said. "You two would love my brownies."

Back upstairs. CLUNK. CLUNK. CLUNK. Into the kitchen. Pans rattled, dishes clanged, and the brownies were baking. Pat hurried back downstairs to check the laundry, rescue the tennis shoes, and refill the soft-drink glasses. Racing upstairs, she checked the brownies.

Finally, wide-eyed, Pat drifted back to the living room where I was now looking at photos of the Asian waterways. She sat down.

"Pat." I put my magazine down and placed a comforting hand on her knee. "I don't know what you're going to do, but I've got to go to bed. Besides, honey, they aren't going to do anything in that basement that you and I didn't do."

"Brownies! More brownies!" she screamed.

What behavioral scientists and mental health experts have long known but have failed to tell us is that parenting teenagers is the number one cause of temporary insanity in the United States. While teenagers are going through rapid changes, their parents are spinning around, frantically trying to decide how to act and react.

Not that there aren't plenty of happy times in raising teenagers. Who will ever forget a daughter getting ready for the school play? Or a son singing in the church youth group? Or the hope we felt rise up when they left to serve as camp counselors?

But we also remember the first time they wrecked the car, ran up a sky-high phone bill, got into trouble at school, and refused to speak to the family for a week.

It's tough to be a teenager.

And it's almost as hard to be the parent of one. These are disruptive years, and we look for easy answers but we don't find many. The best we can do is gather information, put our best instincts to work, and ask God for enough patience to tame a tiger.

Smart parents learn. They collect facts, they talk to other parents, they listen to their teenagers, they read books, they take classes. Smart parents aren't too proud to admit they need help, and they find the resources for knowledge and encouragement.

There Is Hope

Raising teenagers isn't a win or lose situation. Don't look for black or white, A or F, success or failure. Parents who establish goals for their children are usually frustrated. Young people have a way of setting their own targets and hitting them in their own way.

One set of parents felt they had failed because their children didn't attend Sunday evening church. Another couple was discouraged because their teenager didn't go to college. A third parent griped because her teen wore her hair too short.

Too often we concentrate on the trees and lose sight of the proverbial forest. The real goal of parenting should be to help our children become who *they* think they should be, not what *we* think they should be. Parents who try to help, without controlling, eventually regain their sanity.

The most exciting part about teenagers is that they are people who are worth knowing. They aren't objects or possessions. Neither are they mere "reflections" of their parents.

Teenagers are individuals as fascinating as any kaleidoscope, and yet as simple as smooth stones. They are people. And God has placed them in our care for a few short years. So dive into the challenge with all the enthusiasm you can muster, and keep a tight grip on your sanity. You may need it along the way.

1

The Physical Explosion

Like many parents I wasn't at all prepared for the onset of adolescence. I enjoyed our relationship with the children through grade school. They knew less history than I did and we were about even in English and math. So I felt equal to the task and actually looked forward to roaring into the teen years with our three children.

But when our oldest child crossed the sound barrier into teendom, it was like a spaceship had torn through the living room. One day Mary was a pleasant, idealistic, cooperative little girl, and the next day she hissed and growled like a cornered bobcat.

My only regret is that I didn't see it coming. Bewildered and confused I wondered what had happened to my little girl. Both Mary and I could have been saved a great deal of grief if someone had simply said, "Don't worry, Bill; it's normal."

This chapter is addressed to every parent who needs to know "it's normal." The big change into

adolescence may be stressful, it may be unpredictable, it may be frustrating, but above all else, most
of it is normal.

The physical and emotional changes that take
place during the teen years are what we call adolescence. It is the long transition between childhood and adulthood. This change can begin as
early as nine years of age and usually ends by the
early twenties.

We will be better able to respond to the needs
of our teenagers if we understand the differences
between children and adolescents and the causes
behind this transition. Smart parents learn what to
expect and share that information with their
emerging teenagers. The physical changes that take
place are often both frustrating and confusing for
an adolescent, and will trigger the emotional in-
stability so common with this age group. Preparing
your child, and yourself, for puberty will help ease
the transition.

The Changes Are Unpredictable

The exact age at which each physical change
will occur is hard to predict precisely. Some children develop slowly, others rapidly.

It is important for parents to be reassuring by
reminding the young person that height, weight,
foot size, breast size, ear size all grow unevenly,
and most of us are later pleasantly surprised at our
adult proportions.

Teenagers frequently worry over where they
will fit in among their peers. Comparisons and crit-
icisms are common with this age group. Many adolescents also worry that their physical changes,

or lack of them, will determine their future acceptability.

As parents we can't totally eliminate these fears, but we can help. If we admit that we were "late bloomers" or we express our admiration for short or chubby people, we create a feeling that all sizes are normal. Praising people for their unique personality or emotional maturity, rather than physical characteristics, will help emphasize to your child what is really important in an individual.

While we can't erase all adolescent fears, we can supply information for their computers. That information will help them process their self-image as they grow.

The Puberty Change Table

Remember, these changes are what occur in most adolescents in the following general order, but because we are all unique individuals the timing and order may vary considerably.

Female	Male
growth of pubic hair	growth of penis
breast development	growth of testicles
onset of menstrual period	growth of facial hair
	growth of pubic hair
development of hips and pelvis	sweat-gland development
vagina growth and secretion	height increase
height increase	deepening of voice
sweat-gland development	strength development
growth of facial hair	

The two areas most adolescents are concerned about center on timing and size. They want to know when the changes will occur and what the final results will be. Comparisons become very important in a teenager's search for normalcy and peer acceptance.

Teenagers receive much of their security from their parents. When a parent is knowledgeable and relaxed during his or her child's puberty, the young person is more likely to be at ease. If a parent expresses anxiousness over the child's height, chubbiness, thinness, or extra hair, for example, the teenager tends to go into orbit, too.

Parents need information and then a calm attitude. If a parent believes breast size is important, for example, and conveys that anxiety to their teenage daughter, she will pick up on that concern and her own worries will increase dramatically.

This is an excellent time to check our own value system. Too often Christians fall into the same secular trap as the rest of the world. We give the impression that tall people are more important than short people. We tout athletes as more valuable than non-athletes. Society has set an impossible standard for physical characteristics, and provided our teenagers with a shallow and shaky value system that is bound to fail them.

One of the best gifts we can give to our teenagers is a role model of solid Christian values. We must communicate our conviction that no human being is more or less valuable because of size or appearance. This basic attitude of acceptance will provide a strong and lasting foundation on which our children can build their self-esteem. Give your teen confidence of his or her intrinsic value in Christ.

The Ripple Effect

Puberty is not something that happens exclusively to young people—it is a change that affects the entire family. When eleven-year-old Angela begins menstruating, look for changes in eight-year-old Matthew and forty-year-old Dad. Try to be understanding and reassuring to everyone in the home.

If Angela turns grumpy or irrational at times, her mood swings take a toll on Matthew. If she is suddenly snappy toward her parents, they may be tempted to react in a negative way. Angela is not an island. It is somewhat like what happens when Dad or Mom loses their job—the entire family experiences repercussions.

Puberty doesn't exactly require intensive care, but it can knock the family out of sync. Eliminate confusion by explaining what is going on to the teen, and then to family members. Be open to respond to each person's needs as the family goes through this transition. (One parent may need to help the other understand what is happening, and one or both parents will need to explain and be available to the other members of the family.)

2

Four Needs Never Change

There are certain fundamentals about youth that do not change from generation to generation. Youth is a transitional period and certain facts remain true about the changes that take place.

When a young person says "You don't understand," adults may feel insulted. We think that going through the teen years is like riding a bike—regardless of how long it's been, once you get on, it all comes back.

The frustrated young person throws up his hands in despair because he can't seem to get through to his "aging" parents. He doesn't think they can possibly know what he is going through. In a sense he is right, because everyone's perspective varies. However, there are some constants that remain from generation to generation. Your teenager needs to know that his/her parents swam those same rapids, especially when it comes to seeking the answers to four of life's questions:

1. Who am I?
2. Does anyone love me?
3. Who is God?
4. Where do I fit in with my friends?

Who Am I?

We all did it. We stared in the mirror, fretting about our nose or facial structure; we combed our hair incessantly, and worried about our ears—too big, too small, evenly set? Turning our face from left to right, we wondered which side was our best profile. Did we look like Tom Cruise, Mariah Carey, the girl next door, or Ronald McDonald?

As teenagers, our looks were especially important because they were clues to our identity. Were we to become among the fair and favored, those naturally endowed with beauty, or would we need to work at it to avoid being a complete nobody in life?

As younger children, we found much of our identity in our parents. We wanted to be close to them, please them, even mimic them. But the teenager finds his/her identity by separating from their parents.

When a teen is asking himself the question, "Who am I?" he means "in comparison to his peers." When he asks himself, "Do I want to be like my parents?" his inward response is "Definitely not."

When my son, Jim, was nine I went with him to pick out a pair of glasses. I was impressed that he selected a pair of frames exactly like mine. But when Jim was fourteen, nothing about him resembled my choice in apparel.

For most teenagers this is the beginning of the big "rebellion" or separation, the search for independence. If they remain like their parents, they feel as if they are remaining like children—parroting what they see and hear. By pushing off from their parents they are simply seeking their own identity.

How many teenagers will admit that they like their parents' type of music, even if it isn't too bad? Who wants to sit and watch the news with Dad? How often does a teenage girl ask to borrow her mother's blouse? The average teen has a driving, natural need to become themselves—a unique individual. They don't want to be lost in their parents' world, and they aren't eager to have their parents trekking around in theirs.

The search for who they are goes on throughout their teen years and often longer. Some of us never complete the hunt. At forty we are frequently asking the same introspective questions we asked at fourteen.

Does Anyone Love Me?

Teenagers aren't sure they are lovable. Lovableness is at the heart of the issue, and outward appearance is all-important in his or her mind.

Does anyone care what happens to a rapidly changing, stringy-haired, awkward adolescent? Is there a boy or girl out there who will say they think I am even remotely cute?

This is part of the reason why teenagers push their parents away. The girl with facial blemishes believes she is ugly and highly undesirable. She insults her parents and tries to separate herself from them. By acting obnoxious she is really asking her parents if they love her. A teenage son may act repulsively to disgust his parents and chase them away. If his parents react negatively and reject him, his worst fear is confirmed—he is pond scum and even his parents agree.

If, however, parents show and maintain their love for their teens while they act unlovely, they are saying in effect that the teen has value. He is lovable. The teen pushed them away and they refused to leave.

A fourteen-year-old argued with his dad and suddenly blurted, "Why don't you throw me out?" He was testing his father. The boy felt useless and wanted to see if his dad agreed. Wisely, his father refused to do such a thing, and thereby made the teenager feel wanted.

When your teen pushes you away, he/she usually wants you to stay—at least be available. Later they will be grateful for the immovable parent.

Who Is God?

This may come as a shock to some, but teenagers tend not to be the raving pagans that many adults imagine. They may not know how to express their faith, and their beliefs may not be fully entrenched or maturely sorted out, but many teens long for a spiritual connection.

The most important piece of evidence is that more people accept Christ as Savior while a teenager than at any other age. This has been true as long as statistics have been kept on the subject.

Another evidence of teens' interest in spiritual things is seen in the gifts that they most often give one another. I have always been amazed at how many crosses on chains and religious plaques and mementos are exchanged among young people. They seem to value their relationships enough to want God to have some influence in them.

We could go so far as to say that teenagers are more interested in spiritual matters, on the average, than their adult counterparts. Again, they may not be comfortable expressing their faith, but that doesn't mean it doesn't run deep.

With so many changes going on in their lives, young people long for something that is changeless. A solid rock. Their fear of being unacceptable makes them more receptive to the offer of unconditional love that is in Christ.

I know this was true for me. As a fifteen-year-old with almost no church background, I was astonished to hear about a love with no strings attached. To think that Jesus Christ would accept me as I was, love me, and forgive me was an amazing discovery.

This does not mean that every young person is chomping at the bit to become a Christian. What it does suggest is that there is a sizeable number who want exactly what faith in Christ has to offer.

Where Do I Fit in With My Friends?

Closely related to "Who am I?" and "Does anyone love me?" is the social need for friendship among peers. We are social creatures and our need to be connected to others is naturally strong.

As a teen loses his first identity with his parents, he looks for a new identity within his peer group. This drastic, lateral movement can be earth-shaking for everyone.

What kind of choices in friends will they make? Who will they hang out with? What kind of influence will these friends have on them?

Teenagers instinctively know they cannot remain tied to their parents. But they need someone to be in "their nest," so to speak. Who will it be? They begin to match themselves with friends who are willing to bond with them.

Anyone who can remember having once been a teenager will recognize the four basic needs, or life questions, cited at the beginning of this chapter. If we, as parents, can anticipate and identify these questions and struggles as they come to our teens, we will be better equipped to relate to them during this confusing, chaotic time in their lives.

3

Developing Teen-Esteem

Caught in the void between childhood and adulthood, teenagers struggle with finding their identity in the world of young adults, and are often left with feelings of inadequacy. As grade-school children, they were intent on imitating and pleasing their parents, and feelings of acceptance and value were the rewards of their behavior. But when young teens throw off everything associated with childhood, they are left in a sort of behavioral gap, and their self-esteem tends to take a deep, fast dive.

This drastic decrease in feelings of worth and value accounts for many of the problems a young person faces. Their challenges are increasing daily while their confidence to handle those challenges is deflating like a punctured balloon.

In many cases, girls seem to fare worse than boys. The idealistic, steady, studious, dependable eleven-year-old girl will frequently turn into a thirteen-year-old who is anxious, uneven, fearful, and self-deprecating.

The following are three major reasons why teen-esteem plummets:

1. *Rapid Body Change*

Am I a child or an adult? Their body says they are neither. In the spring they are short; by next winter they are tall. The changes in their bodies come about at an uneven rate when compared to their peers, leaving young people feeling out of control and off balance.

2. *Self-Consciousness*

Frequently, when discussions center on them, thirteen-, fourteen-, and fifteen-year-olds want to hide. Already feeling awkward and self-conscious, comments about how they have "grown" or are becoming "quite the young lady" (or young man) make young teens want to disappear.

Because they reject much about themselves, they assume everyone else rejects them, too.

3. *Peer Integration*

Mix the first two insecurities: a changing body and self-consciousness; then toss a hundred teens together at school and the result is chaos. While their self-worth is running weak, they are expected to discover their identity and accomplish great feats during the next several years.

Who am I? Am I accepted? Am I an athlete? Am I a scholar? Am I an insider? An outsider? A rebel? A conformist?

Within this swirling scene, teenagers often lose confidence in themselves and their own goals and

run the risk of becoming people they don't want
to be.

The Dangers of Low Teen-Esteem

Picture yourself in a situation where your bills
are rapidly increasing while your income is de-
creasing. You are expected to make ends meet
when the odds are against you.

Teenagers face similar situations of stress. At a
time when they may feel increasingly inadequate,
they must meet the challenges of schoolwork, extracurricular activities (such as sports), peer pressure to conform, and parent pressure to excel.

The teen's ability to interact in a healthy manner with his peers is largely dependent upon his
self-concept and capacity to maintain an individual identity. If a teen has plummeting self-esteem,
he is apt to act less rationally. He either works too
hard to fit into a certain group of friends or he
drops out of the crowd and becomes a hostile
loner. Either can be a volatile situation.

A teen that is insecure may try to move into a
particular peer group in a desperate attempt to feel
accepted. In this quest he may resort to unreasonable extremes, such as buying clothes he can't afford; rebelling against his parents; abusing alcohol
or drugs; compromising his beliefs and moral values. Untold damage can result as teenagers try to
discover where they fit in among their peers.

Others, convinced they can't move into an established group, quit trying and drop out of the
social scene. They may decide to become anti-
social and resort to unacceptable behavior. Their
energies might turn from school and church func-

tions to a general refusal to participate in anything they perceive as acceptable established behavior.

Both the social climber and the social drop-out suffer from the same problem. They aren't comfortable with their own image. They don't like the person in the mirror. If asked if they are happy with who they are, the answer would be a resounding *no.*

Struggling to become either an insider or an outsider is merely the mask for a major identity crisis. Unfortunately, too many teens are hurt in the normal attempt to discover who they are.

Some examples are when young people try to swap sex for love; alcohol or drugs for acceptance; expensive clothes or questionable behavior for popularity. Sometimes parents make the devastating mistake of actually urging their teen on in bizarre pursuits to become accepted by a particular crowd.

Self-worth cannot be attained by certain actions or connections with the right people. This wrong attitude only results in an insecure, unhappy young person in designer jeans.

How Parents Can Help

Be forewarned: You may, as a parent, have done everything "right" in raising your child, and attempted to build confidence in your teen, but he or she *still* might struggle with low self-esteem. There are no secret formulas, no sure-fire ways to produce confident, well-adjusted young people. It is a very complex time of life. Don't accept the burden upon yourself of making your teen feel worthwhile. Instead, strive to provide loving, positive reinforcement.

1. *Work on Your Own Self-Esteem.*

We need to be sure we have a healthy sense of self-worth. Jesus Christ gives us value. Our value isn't based on what others think of us, or on what we have been able to accomplish in life. If we feel confident of our value in Christ, we reflect that value to our children.

2. *Reinforce Your Teen's Value.*

Parental acceptance is important, even if your teen may give you the impression that it is not. Compliment your teenager honestly and often, and express your happiness in them as individuals. Don't let the home ever be a place of rejection—they get plenty of that other places. The family environment should be one of unconditional love and acceptance. *Encourage! Encourage! Encourage!* This is tough to do, especially if your own parents were not an encouragement to you, but it *is* possible. Ask God for extra grace to be a positive influence and encouragement to your teen.

3. *Change Your Vocabulary.*

To joke about the teen years or to speak disparagingly of teenagers is unacceptable, especially when speaking around our young people. Don't make them feel any more odd than they already feel. It can only be harmful to their fragile self-esteem.

4. *Give Your Teenagers Choices and Responsibilities.*

Gradually shift the responsibility for your teens' making their own decisions and choices over a period of time. Don't expect them to be able to assume this all at once. Give teens more and more areas where they can safely use their own judgment. For example: Allow them to launder their own clothes, clean their own bedroom, clean a bathroom, or vacuum a room. Let them take the car to get the oil changed; get estimates when they dent the bumper. You don't protect your teens by taking responsibility away from them. Assure them that you are confident of their ability to handle the additional load. And if they make a mistake, and they will, don't take back the responsibilities you've given. Make them accountable for their mistakes. Encourage them; support them; but don't bail them out.

Again, don't dump everything on them too quickly. Too much responsibility at once may drown what little self-esteem they have. Shift choices and responsibilities gradually, starting when the teen is in the thirteen to fifteen age range, and keep in mind that your young adult should be making almost all his own choices by the time he is ready to leave home.

5. *Don't Make the Family Teen-Centered.*

By this we mean sacrificing or neglecting the needs of other family members in favor of the needs of the teenager, simply because they appear to be so outstanding. If this happens, the teen will have trouble learning to appreciate and respect others, creating a false sense of importance about themselves. If teenagers are made to feel that they are the center of the family universe, they are being set up for a collapse.

True self-esteem includes adequate esteem for

others. The needs of each person in the family must be considered. The biblical admonition is that we not think of ourselves more highly than we ought to think (Romans 12:3).

4

Help Your Teenager Cope With Frustration

What do adults generally do when life gets tough? We may eat more; watch more TV; take medications; drink more coffee. Some of us go shopping, do woodworking or other hobbies, take long drives, or soak in the tub. Hopefully, over the years we have learned to find ways to deal with our frustrations in socially acceptable fashions.

Despite our maturity and experience, however, some of us still turn to destructive patterns such as screaming, hitting, battering, insulting, smashing, belittling, or other negative responses.

If adults are sometimes poor at coping, how can they expect their young people to do any better? Youth are learning survival skills in a pressure-packed world and it is reasonable to expect them to occasionally behave badly. The best we can do is to strive to be a good example, and then realize that for the teen trial and error, mistakes and successes are going to be the norm. We cannot expect a sixteen-year-old to handle *all* of his problems in a responsible, flawless manner. Let every parent say, "I know my teen will mess up because I am twenty-five years older and I still mess up!"

How Can Teenagers Cope?

When a young person deals with his frustrations, he will find some avenue of coping that will enable him to survive. Parents cannot force a teenager to choose a good method of coping. Neither can they be responsible for which outlets the teen selects. But parents can help by providing as many good and healthy outlets as possible.

Most outlets fall into one of these four categories:

1. Confronting the problem.
   (Study; direct the issue to the one in charge; work it out with friends, family, etc.)

2. Ignoring the problem.
   (Refuse to study; sulk; blame others; give up.)

3. Acting out frustrations.
   (Get into trouble with authorities; steal; drink; skip school; rebel against parents.)

4. Diverting energy.
   (Start a hobby, help a friend, take on a new responsibility.)

Many readers will recall having tried each of these tactics at different times. I can remember working hard and trying to cooperate with school authorities. I can also remember giving up, feeling lost, and barely passing some subjects. At least half of my junior-high experience was spent in the principal's office because I was a great mischief-maker. In high school my schoolwork left me frustrated, so I started the school newspaper and organized a group to feed the hungry.

When a teenager is frustrated, he may weigh the options and go for the outlet with which he feels comfortable, or he may just react out of habit. Sometimes a parent needs to show the teen that there are options—that he or she doesn't have to always respond in a negative manner.

How Can Parents Provide Influence and Help?

Ultimately a teenager must make his own choices. And sometimes the young person with every advantage will follow the wrong path. They come to decisions in ways that even they cannot always explain. Parents are not responsible for the teen's choices, but there are some things they can do that might help.

1. *Be Big on Praise.*

It's easier to cope if you feel that others believe in you. Teenagers receive no greater honor than to have their parents speak well of them. Many of us tell our friends that we are proud of our children, but we fail to tell the teen.

I used to think it would weaken my children if I praised them. That was a mistake with hurtful consequences. Pile praise on them. Approval is a key ingredient to reducing frustration.

I know a man who is an engineer. In his home he has an impressive display of artwork that he has done himself. When asked why he didn't pursue a career as an artist, he said, "When I was fifteen, I showed a drawing of mine to my dad. He merely shrugged his shoulders and walked away. If he had simply told me I'd done a good job, I might have been a career artist today."

Avoid frustrations by providing praise.

2. *Suggest Options.*

When young people don't know where to turn, they need to hear some ideas. They may not respond well to direct commands (most of us don't), but teens soften up when they hear there are choices.

A parent might say, "Who knows, if you don't want to go to college, maybe business school or trade school would be better. What would happen if you worked for a year and then picked a school?"

That same teenager might enroll at Harvard in the fall, but his parents helped remove the frustration by providing options.

Teenagers are far more willing to accept help from parents if they feel they are being trusted to make a wise choice.

3. *Make Yourself Available.*

Although many teenagers have trouble going to their parents for advice, most want to know that their parents are available if they need them.

Availability means a parent is home a reasonable amount of time; has flexible hours and can stay up late with the teen if necessary; will cancel a night out in order to provide a listening ear; is willing to listen to plans and arguments he does not agree with.

Too many parents fantasize that they are approachable when in fact they are not. It costs something to be available, but its value is immeasurable.

4. *Furnish a Set of Values.*

A frustrated teen is often the one who didn't receive a set of workable values. We usually discuss the problems created by too many stringent rules, but the difficulties that arise from no boundaries can be even greater.

We are told to train up a child in the way he should go. Our failure to supply those guidelines leaves a young person powerless to cope with a threatening world. A rudderless youth will feel lost at sea.

None of us can entirely erase a young person's frustrations. Nor should we try. The best we can do is to seek to understand why they are having trouble coping and then provide them with healthy outlets. As parents, we can be a haven, a support for our teens during these tumultuous years.

5

Ten Conversation Starters

How many of us have sat at the dinner table and tried to get a tongue-tied teenager to talk? As parents we try our best to be hip and tuned in to the young people's wavelength, but we barely get grunts and nods in return. We hear plenty of complaints about parents who don't talk, but what about the teenager who answers every question with a feeble "yeah," "nah," or an occasional two-syllable "maybe."

That's the way it was at our house anyway. Finally our daughter, Mary, decided to put an end to all this fruitless conversation. One evening she simply brought a book to the dinner table and escaped into the safe world of literature.

I was livid. *The nerve,* I thought, *of a testy teenager shutting out her parents by hiding behind a novel.* Didn't she realize that these were important years when we needed to connect and share our wisdom? I forbade her to ever bring a book to the table again. However, the missing book didn't improve our conversations.

What's the problem? Why do most parents have trouble engaging their youth in good dialogue? Why are some parents more successful at it than others?

To find some answers I talked to teenagers about how to start a conversation. Between our own experience and the suggestions teenagers gave me, a few remarkable patterns began to appear.

Obstacles to Good Conversation

Brad said, "I'll never tell my parents about any real problems. If I say too much to them, they just take over and run everything. I'd rather keep it to myself."

1. *We must relax our hand of authority if we expect a teenager to confide in us.*

One of our biggest problems as adults is that we only see ourselves as authority figures. We want our teenagers to open up to us and share their personal feelings; but if we don't approve of what they say, we put the heat on.

On the one hand we say "go ahead and talk," while with the other we make a fist in case they say what we don't want to hear. It's like a patrolman asking you if you were speeding. He doesn't want you to say you weren't.

Another obstacle is our seeming need to criticize. It has been said that the average conversation between an older teenager and his parents consists mostly of criticism. The teenagers I talked to agree that this is generally true.

2. *Continuous criticism will kill conversation.*

It makes sense. As parents we are frustrated because our teens won't talk to us. When we finally get into a conversation with them, we figure we had better correct a few things while we have their attention. Who knows when this opportunity may come again? So we throw in, "Is your bedroom clean?" "Did you do your homework?" and "How's your grade coming in math?"

3. *Conversation takes time to cultivate, like a garden.*

Parents are generally in a hurry. Consequently, they tend to want short, concise conversations, but expect them at the same time to be deep, revealing, and personal—almost an impossible combination. Statistics show that most fathers spend only three minutes a day talking to their children. Almost all the teenagers I spoke to said this is fairly accurate.

Instant rapport with anyone, no less our teenagers, is a pipe dream. We are looking for something like a microwave conversation. We want to punch up three minutes on the timer and start sharing with each other, expecting instant understanding and camaraderie.

It's hard to hold a meaningful conversation with someone we don't know. In the case of our teenagers, we have usually failed to learn their interests, their hobbies, their culture, their music, or other things that are important to them.

4. *The gift of good conversation is the ability to listen.*

Good talkers must first be good listeners. Parents need to convince their teenagers that they care about what they think. Any sign of impatience or superficial interest will shut the relationship down.

I can remember trying to engage our son, Jim, in conversation. Immediately when I was done talking I expected him to either reply, confess, or make an in-depth statement. When he didn't respond immediately, I began to bark at him.

If I could do it over again I would wait longer for his response. We could have sat silently. He should have had time to mull it over and join the conversation at his own speed.

We have built obstacles that we can't even see. They are like glass walls. Until we admit they exist and begin to dismantle them, meaningful conversation is unlikely.

Create the Atmosphere

A sophomore girl told me, "Conversation can't just begin at the supper table. Parents have to be close to us the rest of the time if they expect us to start talking at the table."

If there is friction between family members, there is little likelihood that healthy, spontaneous conversation will take place. Try to mend fences; get to know each other; develop trust. Teenagers need friendly parents. They don't necessarily expect or want parent-friends, but friendly parents are a possibility.

Teenagers prefer informal settings for engaging

in conversation with their parents. They don't like family conferences or twenty questions at the dinner table. A casual atmosphere, like the kitchen or family room, is more natural and more comfortable for everyone.

Standing around in the kitchen during meal preparation, for instance, got high marks by both males and females. It's a setting in which they don't feel trapped or on the spot. They can either change the topic or leave if they need to.

Don't subject your teen to anything that resembles a police interrogation. Not many of us would open up and take conversational risks in that kind of atmosphere. Although there may be times when interrogation is called for, don't expect much response. The minute they feel under the gun, teenagers reach into their bag of evasive skills and begin to dodge the questions they don't like.

Work on your relationship with your teens before you expect profitable conversation. People who aren't getting along don't communicate.

Everyone is more likely to open up at a ball game, on a shopping trip, or out to dinner. One of our family's favorite outings was to go to the coffee shop. Relaxing, munching on bread sticks, and sipping a soft drink helped our teenagers and ourselves to open up. No agenda. We weren't fishing for inside information. Just shooting the breeze, letting the conversation flow. It helped us learn a great deal about one another as we explored subjects we never anticipated discussing.

Ask Broad Questions

When conversation becomes too pointed, young people tend to get uncomfortable. Suspicion gets the best of them and they wonder what their parents are digging for. A question like "How's school?" is wide open. It allows the teen to pick out a part of school life they enjoy and start talking about it. But when you ask "How's algebra?" you have narrowed the subject and, especially if your teen is having trouble with algebra, he is more likely to be irritated. It's a loaded question rather than a conversation starter.

If we are intent on only bringing up unpleasant subjects, our discussions will be very minimal. Notice that questions about homework lead to one-word or short-sentence responses. They usually go like this:

"Got any homework?"

"Nope!"

"How can that be? You've got some really tough subjects."

"Did it in school."

With that the young person darts out of the room and is gone. What happened? The opening question was

1. Too narrow
2. Too unpleasant
3. Too interrogative

The teen has little motivation to continue this conversation. Almost no information is shared, no understandings are reached, and the parent is locked out. This isn't to say that parents should never ask about homework. However, it is to say that homework is not usually a great way to jump-start a conversation.

A broad statement like "If you need any help

with your homework, I'm available" can be an open, warm invitation for dialogue.

Conversation Openers

1. *"What's going on?"*

Broad, nonjudgmental, inviting. Allows the teen to talk about anything he wants to.

2. *"Your hair looks nice." "I like the music you're playing." "Your room looks great."*

Compliments make the teen feel good about him/herself.

3. *"How's your hobby coming along?"*

Know what your teen's interests are and ask about them.

4. *"What's happening with the basketball team?"*

Show an interest in sports or activities that your teen is involved in at school.

5. *"Anything new about that drug bust at school?"*

Be broad. Show concern; don't ask for names, or sound like the police sent you.

6. *"That new girl you brought over seems nice."*

Ask about friends in an approving manner. Don't pry.

7. *"How's school going?"*

Your tone of voice is important. Ask follow-up

questions only after the young person replies.

8. *"That jacket looks really comfortable."*

Ask about their clothes. Be accepting, nonjudgmental about their choice of apparel.

9. *"What kind of music do you like best?"*

Show an interest in music or other forms of entertainment they may be into at the moment.

10. *"If you were the math teacher, would you give homework?"*

Opinion questions are hard to turn down. They don't sound like quizzes. Teenagers are pleased when someone respects their views in an area where they have experience.

Meaningful conversation is based on two people who trust each other within a safe atmosphere. If parents will try to keep certain guidelines in mind, they might be able to develop dialogue that will create understanding and even healthy friendship with their teenagers.

6

Can You Trust Your Teenager?

For many parents the subject of trust comes up when the teenager is standing at the door about ready to leave for the evening. She has her coat on and her ride is waiting outside. No curfew has been predetermined, and suddenly it becomes necessary to tell her what time she should be in.

Why are we surprised when our daughter says, "You don't trust me, do you?"

Leaving such instruction or information till the last possible moment puts you, the parent, in a kind of trap. You have to come up with a clever but accurate reply to the question of trust.

If you answer, "Of course I trust you," she may snap back, "Then why can't you trust me for an extra hour?"

On the other hand, if you say, "No, I don't trust you," she understandably replies, "Then what's the use of trying? My own mother doesn't have any faith in me."

It would be good if we didn't have to answer questions like that under volatile conditions. Ideally, curfews and other rules and guidelines should be discussed and determined before the last minute. That's why when there isn't time for discussion, we feel as if we would like to take a couple of days, read a book, listen to a radio show, browse through an article or two, and then give an answer filled with spiritual wisdom. Unfortunately, though, parents don't always have that luxury. Often it's necessary to have a quick, charming, reasonable answer—this instant.

Just in case you have a crisis situation tonight, let me suggest a few replies that may suit the situation. Tailor one or more response with your own words:

- Sometimes I trust you a great deal and other times I feel a little shaky.
- In a situation like the one you're getting into I wouldn't even trust myself.
- Not entirely. We need to sit down and talk about trust.
- Prove I can trust you by being in at the time I requested.
- Trust has nothing to do with it. Midnight is late enough under the circumstances.
- My trust in you is growing all the time. Be here!

The Importance of Trust to a Teenager

When a teenager complains that no one trusts her, there is more behind that statement than the superficial. It is a vital issue.

Let's look at several reasons why the subject of trust comes up at all.

1. *It's a smoke screen.*

Teenagers are bright and resourceful. They know their parents will stumble over the answer. It is an easy trap and diverts the issue of when to be in.

2. *They want their parents to be honest.*

A teenager who is going out into a risky situation doesn't entirely trust himself. He knows it could be dangerous, but he doesn't want to admit that the circumstance may be too difficult for him to handle. He is looking for a parent to draw the line and say, "No, I don't trust anyone in that setting. You can't go."

They want their parents to supply the courage they are momentarily unable to supply for themselves. But if you do take a stand and tell your teen he can't go somewhere, don't expect to be thanked. The teen will no doubt still throw a fit. Although inwardly he may be relieved to be removed from the potentially harmful situation, he will not want to acknowledge that his parents are correct in denying him the opportunity.

3. *They want to see signs of trust.*

When a daughter asks, "Do you trust me?" she would like to hear, "Yes, most of the time, but not always." In that statement she hears that she is generally trustworthy. She hears encouragement, but not foolhardy release. She can then build on the affirmation that her parent trusts her.

If we say we don't trust them at all, we destroy their confidence; but if we say we trust them entirely, we place too much burden on their shoulders.

4. *They want to see trust grow.*

What could be more frustrating for a teenager who always gets good grades than to hear his parent ask every evening, "Do you have your homework done?" The evidence that he handles his academic work well should create trust. When a teenager feels as if he can never please his parents, he will become angry, frustrated, and develop a shaky sense of self-worth.

Likewise, steady, dependable performance should result in added trust. If your teenager never gets into trouble, don't tell him every time he goes out not to get into trouble. What's the point of hassling the kid?

Biblical Guidelines

"Whoever can be trusted with very little can also be trusted with much" (Luke 16:10).

Naturally the message applies to everyone— adults and teenagers alike. When a young person is faithful in taking care of small responsibilities, he may demand that he be trusted with larger decisions and responsibilities. He has a right to expect to be trusted with more when he has handled the smaller tasks well.

"Love . . . always trusts" (1 Corinthians 13:7).

Even after we have been fooled, tricked, let down, duped, hoodwinked, and bamboozled, parents must gather their courage and learn to trust again. Love demands that of us.

It is painful to trust again after we have been terribly disappointed, but love must learn to climb uphill.

"Even my close friend, whom I trusted, he who shared my bread, has lifted up his heel against me" (Psalm 41:9).

Don't be shocked when a teenager lets you down. The best of us do it to each other. That's the human condition. At some point, we have all become disillusioned by the ones we love.

Try not to make a teenager's betrayal bigger than it really is. Most of us flunk the test of trust at some time or other. The key, as parents, is to keep in mind the ultimate goal: building trust and responsibility within our teenagers.

7

Teen Tension

Few adults ever wish they could go back to become a teenager again. While there are many good
memories, those years can also represent a great
deal of hurt, loss, pain, and disappointment. The
goal of most in high school is to graduate and become free. And most are extremely relieved when
it finally happens.

When we become parents we have our own set
of agonies—keeping a good job, paying bills, main-
taining our health, dealing with marital tension,
and raising our children. We tend to forget what
kind of pain teenagers face. We are tempted to min-
imize their problems. The adult world of troubles
is so real that teen troubles seem small or insignif-
icant.

In truth, young people have a multitude of tensions crowding in on them. If we are to understand
them fully, we need to look beneath the surface
and find out what it is that they are facing.

Austin is fourteen, a sophomore at Benson

High. His world is expanding rapidly, requiring him to make some serious choices.

Austin wants to fit in but he isn't sure where. He doesn't like sports that much; his grades are slipping; he feels uncomfortable around girls; drinking and smoking pot sound intriguing but they frighten him; he thinks nicer clothes might help him fit in better.

In addition to his peer struggles, Austin's parents are getting along only part of the time. He has seen them argue before, but now they seem to be in serious trouble. The stability of their marriage worries him.

Austin's problems are average. Millions of teenagers face the same set of pressures daily. A multitude of others have to cope with far worse situations. They are called upon at a tender, vulnerable age to make major, often life-altering decisions, and they have few resources on which to draw.

Tension Isn't Just for Losers

Some imagine that tensions mount the most for those who are failing in school, or who have the least support at home. The fact is that many young people who appear to be well-adjusted at home and excelling in school may feel as much or more pressure as those around them.

In Los Angeles, a fifteen-year-old star Little League pitcher shot himself in the head. He was described as well-liked, successful in baseball, basketball, and soccer. One of his friends said he was "the last person" you would ever expect to take his own life.

A note he left expressed his love for his family, but also referred to his own ugliness, badness, and the burden of keeping up.

Teenagers who aim for the top often suffer more than anyone. How does the president of the Honor Society cope, for instance, when he fails to make the society the next year? When a young girl goes to cheerleaders' camp and still fails to make the team, how does she deal with the disappointment? The unrealized expectation could haunt her for years.

One young person said, "They tested me for the gifted program when I was in fifth grade, but I wasn't good enough." Her failure to make the program blinded her to the fact that she was gifted enough to be tested. Failing to achieve the top was a hard blow that affected her self-esteem even years later.

What Are the Specific Tensions Teens Face?

To discover what major tensions teenagers face today, we went to two sources. First, we asked teenagers themselves. They were in close agreement on what kind of pressures they felt. Our second source was a student of teenagers. His findings were almost identical to what we had heard from the young people.

The following are the major stressors:

1. *Peer Stress*

The real world of teenagers is their circle of peers. Their number one concern is where they fit among other teenagers and how they are accepted. This is an identity issue. They discover part of who they are by mixing with other young people.

As many teenagers told us, getting along with parents is optional, but fitting in with peers is essential.

2. *Parent Tension*

Teens want to please their parents, but not on parental terms. They would like their parents to be proud of what they do, but not if parents dictate what they should do.

Some parents demand too much and hassle their teens constantly. Teenagers find parents easier to disregard and resist than peers. They would rather battle a parent than a friend—parents have to accept them; friends don't.

3. *Sports Pressure*

Especially true of boys, the pressure to excel in sports is now affecting girls also. As sports become more competitive each year, participants feel the pressure mounting. They find a certain identity in athletics, and when some realize that they will never excel, the scars can last a lifetime.

4. *Ethical Battles*

A teenager's desire to keep moral values and Christian standards is a continuous struggle. Life is a jungle filled not only with choices but also with heavy temptations. The first dilemma is to decide what is right or wrong, and this is becoming more difficult as even the church struggles with absolutes. The second problem is to choose whether to follow one's convictions or to go with the crowd.

In no area are teens pushed and pulled more than in the area of moral choices.

5. *Material Things*

How important are brand name tennis shoes? Designer jeans? Fairly important. It's cool to be different, but not too different. While most don't feel the need to be trendsetters, nerdish won't do either.

Teens admit that clothes do not make the person, but they do affect the image (both the image they reflect and their self-image). Many teenagers are willing to contribute a few bucks to the clothes budget in order to climb up an extra notch on the style ladder.

6. *Boyfriend/Girlfriend*

Teens tend to connect their own value to their ability to get along with the opposite sex. It is a high-identity issue. Girls are concerned with whether or not they are asked out. Guys are worried about getting up enough nerve to ask a girl out. What does it mean if you are a senior and have never been on a date? What does a Christian do about the prom?

These questions and concerns have not changed much over the last thirty years. Of course dating or going out regularly with someone does not prove your worth, but many teenagers (and some adults) still think it does.

7. *Appearances*

Every teenager argues with the mirror. Their features are changing and they are extremely anxious to know what the results will be. Each day they are checking for acne, pushing their ears back, and trying to train their hair. This is no small matter. While adults merely announce, "Don't worry about it," teens are busy searching for new freck-les.

Beware: A teen girl is not usually comparing her appearance with her cousin, Tracy. No, she has a photo of a twenty-five-year-old model with expensive teeth, insured hair, and the latest high-tech cosmetics with which to compete. Almost every teenager will fall short of the standards they set for themselves.

8. *Academics*

Teens live in a complex society. Many have trouble deciding exactly how important grades are. With some groups of boys, high grades are a turn-off. They want to get B's because A's make them less acceptable.

There are three sources of pressure to excel: personal goals, teachers, and parents. For some teens, the pressure comes from all three. When one or all of these sources tie the teenager's personal worth to their grades, serious problems result.

9. *Mobility and Money*

At sixteen the stressors often shift. The question of how much a teenager should or shouldn't work becomes a factor. Many teenagers get a job to provide extras and to establish some independence. Others must work to accrue essentials.

These two factors, mobility and money, change the parent/teen relationship forever. And well it should. The teen no longer depends completely on his parents for transportation and finances. The flight from the nest presents its own set of unique problems and pressures. Not only does the teen need to adjust and adapt, it takes a secure, flexible parent to survive this period with a minimum of medication.

Of course these are not all of the stressors. There is hassle over television—what and how much to watch; music—which kind and how loud to listen; church—when and how much to attend and participate; sibling rivalry, care of younger brothers and sisters; extracurricular activities, homework; family outings, relative gatherings; curfews, and a host of others. Each individual will be affected differently by his/her own set of circumstances. What is a problem or pressure point to one teen will not be a problem to another.

Stress in the teen years is nothing new. But most will admit that pressures on today's teens are somewhat multiplied and come in more varieties. The objects of temptation are marketed, electronic, colorized, more readily available, and pitched by professionals. While no teenager wants pity, we can respect the fact that their stressors are enormously powerful.

Tips for Parents

There is no quick fix to alleviate teen tension, but there are some guidelines that might be helpful.

- Teenagers are not children. They encounter real, strong life-changing and life-threatening pressures.
- Take their stresses seriously. Don't shrug them off as something they will outgrow. Some of it they will never outgrow.
- Be ready to listen without criticism. At 2:00

A.M. they may need a parent's ears and understanding.

- Remove all unnecessary pressure. Don't argue over their hairstyle, clothing, shoes, or earrings.

- Provide counter-pressure at the appropriate time. This can be an art. For example, if your sixteen-year-old is under pressure to drink, provide stronger pressure for him not to drink.

- Be willing to learn from your teenager. He knows more about his present situation than you do. Try to see it from his perspective.

- Admit when you are wrong. Let your teenager see that you are human, not another brick wall.

- Allow your teenager the privilege of being right some of the time. He really is right some of the time.

- Share ideas with another parent to see how your approach sounds.

- Don't be afraid to draw a line; just be sure it is worth drawing.

Teen tension, pressure, and stress is a serious mine field. There is potential for a great deal of harm. Young people need supportive, available parents who will take the time to listen to them, seek to understand them, and help them through this difficult time in their lives.

8

Moody and Brooding

In the interest of family harmony, a father placed a mood chart inside the front door. When he arrived home he moved a pin on the chart to indicate his present feelings—he might be happy, grumpy, angry, tired, level-headed, or even generous. Before others approached him they would check the chart to make sure it was safe and timely.

If we were to set up a chart for teenagers, we might want to make it a wheel and install a needle instead of a pin. A young person upon entering the house could simply spin the needle and let it race over all kinds of emotions, landing wherever. The chart would be accurate no matter where the needle stopped. It's common for a teen's moods to change erratically from moment to moment.

A mother asked her teenaged daughter if she wanted pudding or cake for dessert. The daughter asked what kind of pudding. "Chocolate," the mother responded. The daughter objected, claiming her mother never made vanilla pudding. "I'll make vanilla next time," the mother obliged.

"Yeah, right," the daughter said sarcastically, "you only make what I want when I insist on it. Nobody knows or cares what I like around here."

The mother shook her head and thought, *All this because I asked what she wanted for dessert?*

Similar conversations could be recorded in homes across America. Mother gets hit by teenage mood swing. It defies all logic, is totally out of proportion, and frequently is unpredictable. Nevertheless, it is real, and parents need to learn to make allowance for it.

Mood swings are not simply excuses to be rude. Teenagers are in the midst of physical, mental, and emotional changes over which they have little control. It's hard to remain on an even keel when the boat keeps rocking back and forth.

You can tell a young person to get hold of himself, but often he doesn't know how to do that. He surprises himself with his reactions and feelings. He doesn't always know if he is acting in a mature or immature manner. He wants to be accepted, but he usually feels rejected. Turmoil is a good word for what is going on. If someone has trouble sorting out his thoughts and feelings, he is bound to be uncomfortable with himself, and people who are uncomfortable with themselves are usually awkward around others.

A Bundle of Contributors

Picture a washing machine with a window. Stuff the following components into the washer:

- a rapidly changing body

- a new thinking process
- shifting social patterns
- four boxes of junk food
- a developing sexual awareness
- pressure to conform
- pressure to excel

Now close the door and turn on the machine. What you have tumbling end over end and blending together is a teenager. No wonder they have mood swings.

When we talk about mood swings we aren't talking about bad behavior. All of us on the planet are responsible to deal with bad habits and behaviors that are socially unacceptable. We can only hope to help our teens cope with their mixed emotions and confused thoughts so that they do not express their frustrations in disastrous ways.

How Can a Parent Help?

Help is all we can do. If we could stop teen mood swings we would be candidates for the humanitarian award. At best we can mitigate its effects on everyone involved.

The most important key for parents is never to take away a teenager's choices when it comes to his own feelings. Statements like, "You'd better forgive her," or "Stop seeing him right now," or "You shouldn't feel that way," or "Stop being so moody," are nonproductive.

Better to contribute suggestions, and let the teen make the final decision: "Maybe you'd like to try this . . ." or "Have you ever thought of. . . ?" or "What if you simply stayed away from her the rest of the week? See how you feel about it on Monday.''

Most of us are unlikely to express our true feelings to people who try to take over. We are looking for options and choices, not commands.

Teenagers hurt as they sail through the seas of emotional upheaval. Unfortunately, many have few anchors to hold them steady. Each deserves a good parent or two who are willing to hold on to them.

9

Center Stage

As a teenager, I clearly remember thinking that parents of small children must hope that their children would grow up to be like me. If that sounds terribly egotistical, it was. Years later I discovered that most of those parents barely knew I was alive, and the others gave me almost no thought at all. But teenagers typically see themselves as on center stage, everyone looking straight at them to see what they will do next. (Some of us carry that perception with us long after adolescence.)

Contrast that to what our daughter Mary told us after she entered college. She said she suddenly realized that if she stayed in her room, didn't eat meals, and didn't go to class, no one on campus would even know or care. All eyes were not centered on her. To most people there she was merely a name and number.

One of the chief characteristics of teenagers is their ego-expansion or self-consciousness. As children they felt as if they had the power to make things happen, but they knew they were connected to their families. As teenagers they are becoming more individualistic and tend to interpret every event in terms of how it will affect them.

"All the world is a stage" and teens see themselves as the leading actors. If they gain five pounds they believe everyone will not only notice the change but will talk about it. A "bad hair day" is a tragedy because they think everyone, from the principal to the school cook, is going to make fun of them.

Believing yourself to be on center stage creates a lot of pressure. The spotlights are bright and hot and they show up every blemish. No oddity or imperfection can hide under the relentless glare. Because the teen believes he is under this much scrutiny, each day can be tension-packed.

Embarrassed by Parents

With this much pressure, teenagers can't afford to have an imperfect parent hanging around. In the fourth or fifth grade they thought their mother was beautiful. When they reached the eighth grade they wanted to hide her in the basement.

Parents are either too short, too fat, too bald, or too poorly dressed, and they drive an old, dull car. Teens want their parents to prepare a party—furnish the soft drinks, chips and dip, and other goodies, and then disappear from sight until all their friends go home.

The last thing they want is for their parents to tell jokes, pull pranks, or tell stories about when they were young. Occasionally, under guarded circumstances, they may exhibit moments of pride, like showing off Dad at a father-daughter banquet, for example. They also like to have one or two parents sit in the back of the auditorium during an awards ceremony.

It could be called the great Parent-Teen Square Dance. While the music is playing, a parent is never quite sure when to cut in and when to cut out. The tendency is for parents to take this exclusion personally. They think their teen doesn't like them. More than likely this is not true. Your teen likes you, he just doesn't know what to do with you. Because he can't control you—your hairstyle, the way you dress—or write a script for you to read at appropriate times, he is uncomfortable having his parent around, especially when peers are present.

Remember, the teenager is suffering more agony than his parents and he is twice as bewildered. Try not to lose your cool or collapse into self-pity while this transition is going on. There will come a time when your teen will appreciate you and exhibit pride in you. Be patient.

The Average Teen's Vantage Point

Naturally not every teen is totally self-centered. Many volunteer to help in hospitals, at youth camps, churches, and many other places of service. But the facts do not change the rules. More often teens are concerned with how events affect their own lives at the present.

If a teen's parents divorce, for instance, his first reaction may be one of self-pity. *What a terrible time to get divorced!* he thinks. It is his junior year and he has important things to do. What about the junior/senior banquet? How will he ever get a car if his father moves out? Who will pay for his clothes and what about the new stereo?

Frequently a teen will jump right over his parents' problems, his grandparents' problems, and his siblings' problems. If a relative is gravely ill, the young person may be worried about how this will wreck his weekend.

You may be thinking, don't adults feel self-centered, too, even though they may not admit it? Don't some men get upset when family sickness forces them to cancel a golf date? What's the difference? The difference is that adults *should* have, and generally do have a more encompassing, caring, sacrificial attitude, just by reason of experience and maturity. Most teenagers are not yet capable of seeing beyond their own immediate needs.

Teenage Jugglers

Try to imagine a teenager on center stage juggling five crystal goblets. His job is to keep all five in the air while he makes clever comments. This takes a great amount of intense concentration.

Suppose while he is juggling, a man in the third row gets his suit coat caught in one of the folding chairs and it starts to rip. Soon the man's wife and friends begin helping the man free the garment. They are making a lot of commotion—not intentionally, but because of the circumstances.

What is the young juggler to do? He perceives someone is having trouble, but we don't expect him to stop juggling because someone in the third row has a problem, even if it's his dad.

The juggler sees his job as primary, all-consuming. If he allows anything to break his concentration, the goblets will come crashing to the ground.

A teenager often feels he is juggling all he can manage, and he can't afford to look at anyone else's needs. When an aunt gets sick, the young person is afraid to drop everything and rush to her side. That's when he is likely to scream those familiar words: "Doesn't anybody care what happens to me?"

As they mature, however, they are usually able to pull in the crystal goblets and respond to the people they love.

Don't Be Surprised

If a teenager does respond sympathetically when a relative is critically ill, when Dad loses his job, or when parents are separated, be grateful. But don't be surprised if he reacts insensitively.

Neither should we be surprised if a teenager rejects help from his parent or any other adult. He may wish someone would lighten his load. He may also wish that someone would give him advice on how to handle all that he carries. But he is reluctant to accept help because of certain fears.

One fear is that an adult may not only give advice, but take away the act that is working for him. Teenagers have a gigantic fear that if they ask an adult for help the adult will take over. Remember, he is striving for independence, even though he is on shaky ground. He doesn't see the adult as his equal yet.

A second fear is that if they stop doing what they're doing to learn a better way, their act might fall apart. What they're doing is working for them, even if they are experiencing pain. They are afraid to let go.

Being on center stage is a difficult position to be in. It is a high-tension, unrealistic world. Nevertheless, it is possible for teens to walk out of the spotlight for short periods of time and care very much for others.

10

Playing the Rebel

The role of the rebellious teenager isn't always fun because the act of breaking away can be terribly painful. Rebelling means you climb walls, swim upstream, go against the grain, leap out of nests, disobey orders, and suffer the consequences.

Our daughter Mary told us that she used to drive around the country roads for forty-five minutes after her curfew just to rebel. She had no place to go, nothing to do, bored out of her mind. But Mary was proving to herself that she was a person, an individual. More than just a product of her parents, she had to make sure she was free to become Mary.

Those are hard decisions to follow through on. It isn't easy to drop band class when you know your parents won't understand. You have to face them, explain why you did it (if you know why you did it), and listen to them make you feel like a loser. But you drop the class and take the heat.

And those are only mini-rebellions. Tiny uprisings. Small revolutions. Imagine the pain teen-agers endure when they take gigantic leaps into independence, filled with painful, lasting conse-quences, and have to do major battle with their parents or other authority figures.

Definition of Teenage Rebellion Against Parents

When a parent has expectations for his teenager and that adolescent deviates from those expecta-tions, the teenager is in an act of rebellion. The rebellion might be small (putting his feet on the coffee table) or it could be major (running away with a rock band), but either way it is a deviation from what his parents wanted or expected of him.

If a young person wears a ragged shirt and his parents don't care, that isn't rebellion. Long hair isn't a sign of rebellion unless it contradicts a pa-rental standard. We may see teenagers with pecu-liar behavior, but that doesn't make them rebels. Rebels must be rebelling against a particular set of rules or expectations.

Some teens rebel against all authority, against God, or against society, but that isn't what we are talking about here. What we are specifically con-cerned with is the narrow definition of rebellion against parents.

Rebellion against parents is when a teenager deliberately crosses a line that has been drawn in the sand, even though he has been clearly told not to cross it. In some way, whether slyly, boldly, qui-etly, loudly, or underhandedly, he has knowingly crossed the line. That youth is in an act of rebel-lion.

Why Does a Teenager Rebel?

Reasons for teenage rebellion run anywhere from a simple bad day to a serious personality disorder. Its duration can be from five minutes to the full span of adolescence.

Let's look at some of the most frequent reasons for teen rebellion.

1. *It's an identity thing.*

How will they find out who they are unless they break away from their parents? This simple need is enough to make most teenagers pull away from the harbor. It is natural, even in the best-behaved young person.

2. *The rules are unreasonable.*

Too many parents have rules covering every aspect of life. The parent believes in overbearing authority for authority's sake. They set up a battleground and dare the youth to fight. When his teenager asks, "Why do I have to try out for band?" the parent replies, "Because I said so."

3. *There are no rules.*

A lack of boundaries makes a teenager feel insecure. He wonders if anyone cares whether he succeeds or fails. It's harder to break rules if there are no rules. In order to rebel, this young person has to go to greater extremes.

He may play his music even louder, for instance; or more seriously, have a conflict with the law, use drugs or alcohol—all in a cry for some sort of control. He is rebelling against *lawlessness*. It is a call for walls that he thinks his parents should have provided.

4. *They are mad at the world.*

A "raw deal" teenager feels as though life has been unfair to him. He wishes he were better at sports or academics or better-looking or more popular. Unable or unwilling to deal with his problems, he becomes hostile. Frustrated, and suffering from a sense of low self-worth, he lashes out in rebellion. He wants to make noise, call attention to himself, and express his anger. Often, this person is not upset with the people he takes his anger out on.

5. *They resent their parents.*

Frequently young people become angry at their parents for making them who they are. If they think they are poor or fat or slow or short, the teenager might hold the parent responsible. Most adolescents grow out of this at some point. Others allow the resentment to control them, and they act out their hostilities.

6. *They are avoiding the real problem.*

Picture a teenager getting into trouble with the law because she can't deal with a more serious problem. Inside she is sure that her parents like her brother more than they like her. Unable to complain about that feeling, she shoplifts in the hope that someone will notice how much she hurts.

Imagine another teenager who gets drunk every weekend. He really wishes his father would change his working hours and be home more, but he doesn't feel free to express that. Consequently, he drinks, thinking that will get his father's attention and make him spend time with him.

Both teenagers create more problems because they can't discuss the real problem. Many teenagers may never be able to talk about what is tearing them up.

7. *Who in the world knows?*

Recently a teenager in Nebraska killed his father. It is possible that no one will ever know why he did it. He may not even be sure what forces and decisions came together and caused him to pull the trigger.

When it comes to teen rebellion, two and two don't have to add up to four. Ideal circumstances and good family upbringing that produce a well-balanced teenager in one family will not necessarily create such a person in another.

Some teenagers reject good training and nurturing. Others twist every advantage into disadvantage. That's why parents sit and wring their hands trying to figure out what they did wrong to create such a rebellious teenager.

How to Help a Rebel

Rebel-healing is a tough art and not many of us do it well. But there are some guidelines that might make the rebellion less severe.

1. *Reassess your rules.*

Cut back on rules as the child grows older. Ask if you are trying to apply childhood rules to teenagers. Also ask if you are holding on to old rules that made sense thirty years ago but no longer have merit.

2. *Reinforce the good rules.*

Teenagers need someone to set boundaries and maintain them. It gives them a sense of security, even if they don't admit that. Stand your ground when necessary.

3. *Don't take rebellion personally.*

Parents tend to think disobedience is a personal attack on them. They can feel hurt, insulted, and defensive. Don't make it a battle of wills. If the rule is right, fight for the rule, not your hurt feelings.

4. *Keep trying.*

After you are disappointed a few times, you want to give up. Teenagers need parents who will struggle with them through some terrible conflicts. Parents who refuse to confront only encourage the rebellion. Hold the confrontation to important issues but don't be afraid to discuss problems.

5. *Strive for gradual independence.*

Teenagers need to receive their freedom step-by-step and year-by-year. Letting go is difficult, but it has to be done in a time-release fashion where the youth feels as if he is progressing and is rewarded for what he sees as a growing maturity.

One of the most valuable texts about teenage rebellion is the story of the Prodigal Son in Luke 15. For many parents it is a source of strength, wisdom, and spiritual guidance. As circumstances change, the story gives new insight on freedom, acceptance, forgiveness, and love. It teaches just how little control we have and how much freedom we eventually must give.

Rebellion Is Common in Most Families

Christians often feel crushed when their teens rebel. We have high standards and high hopes for our children and later are dumbfounded when they don't "turn out" just as we had planned. Most families have at least one child who goes through a visible stage of rebellion. Even famous Christian leaders like William Carey, David Livingstone, Billy Sunday, and Billy Graham, to name a few, have had one or more rebellious children.

As painful as it is, we must raise our children to make their own decisions. And sometimes those decisions are not the same ones we would make.

The Rejection Cycle

When my son, Jim, was deep into a rebellious stage, our relationship degenerated into an ugly pattern. I couldn't figure out why, but I noticed that no matter how firmly I reacted, the situation only became worse. He would do the opposite of what I told him, and I became more and more upset with him. After going head to head, his obstinacy only intensified.

Frustrated, depressed, and eating a snack at 1:00 A.M., I suddenly recognized the pattern. Jim would rebel and I would reject him. He would intensify his rebellion and I would double my rejection. By the grace of God I saw that I was rejecting my son, and that is what multiplied the problem. If I was going to war against him, he saw no choice but to increase his war against me.

Finally it dawned on me that one of us had to act like an adult. Since he was not yet an adult, that left me. I decided to get off the rejection cycle.

Correct, Don't Reject

Parents don't have to hide in the corner, frightened to death of what their teenager might do next. We need to stand toe to toe and correct his behavior when necessary. But don't confuse correction with rejection.

Communicate these two facts:

1. You are in total disagreement with their present behavior.
2. You love them anyway.

These two messages are not exclusive. Teenagers can accept the first message and respect their parents, but if they are not reassured of their parents' unconditional love, the young person can become bitter and distance himself further from the family.

Tired of Destructive Behavior

Does a parent have to put up with everything and anything a teen does? The answer is no, but the principle is extreme tolerance. Every parent has to decide how much is too much. When it comes to breaking the law; when drugs, violence, and theft are involved, obviously something has to be done to bring the behavior to a halt. Loving a child unconditionally doesn't mean you let him destroy himself and those around him. There are times when extraordinary action is in order.

Nearly every parent suffers some abuse at the hand of a child. That's the nature of intimacy. We lock on to the people we love and occasionally we get hurt because we care. The alternative is to hold them at a distance for fear we might get hurt.

Acceptance Versus Rejection

We are reminded of the biblical promise that God has accepted us. In spite of our rebellion against Him, God refused to reject us. "While we were still sinners, Christ died for us" (Romans 5:8). We can't earn His love.

"Accept one another, then, just as Christ accepted you, in order to bring praise to God" (Romans 15:7).

Most parents are able to accept their teenagers even under very stressful situations. Put the grace of God to work and be amazed at the strength that is available.

11

The Teen's Life Is Different

There has always been a cultural gap between teenagers and their parents. We all remember our own rebellious years, the disagreements over curfews, clothes, friends. The same arguments go on today, but there is much more involved and the risks are far greater.

Today's teenagers attend schools where there is the potential of meeting armed students, drug pushers, proffered sex, deadly disease, and readily available alcohol. They may also live in neighborhoods that are volatile, and/or come from a shattered home. Over half of the teenagers today live in a divorce situation. Twenty-five percent have single parents, and soon fifty percent will be part of stepfamilies.

A big step toward understanding teenagers is to admit that their world is not exactly like ours was at their age. The surface problems may be similar, but they face deeper and more dangerous conflicts.

The Changes Are Rapid

In our day, change could be compared to watching an ocean liner coming from a distance and then pass slowly by. Today change is like the Concord. It comes out of nowhere and roars past at a shattering speed.

A young person recently told me that when she was in the National Honor Society in high school almost none of the members drank alcohol. They were the group with a reputation for never challenging the rules. Five years later, when her younger sister joined the Society, almost everyone in the group used alcohol.

The change is so rapid and the teen culture so different that a church in the Kansas City area has started "teen" church. Each Sunday after the opening worship, the youth pastor goes with the teenagers into another room to share the message. The form of communication is different, the application is different, the language is different, even though the basic message is the same.

Researchers have suggested that in ten years our world has changed as much as it did in the previous seventy years. That same rate of change could be said of the teen world. If we are still using teenagers of the '70s and '80s as our model, we are playing record albums in the age of the compact disc.

Three Agitations

The average young person experiences rapid change in three aspects of their life:

- school
- physical body
- family

In previous generations we tended to find security in school and family. That left us to fend off the sharks of a changing body and a new identity. Occasionally we had problems in school or at home, but by and large we had a safer, more secure place in which to grow and change.

When the neighborhood bully chased us, we ran home for protection and comfort. We looked forward to school, where we could surround ourselves with friends. Today's teens often go home to an empty house, and the school is not always a safe haven.

Remember when the big offenses at school were chewing gum or running in the halls? Or maybe you passed a note to your girlfriend. When you got home, Mom was usually there baking cookies.

Many adults look back at their teen years with warm memories. We may think it wouldn't be so bad to go back and relive a year or two of those days. Today's teenager will probably remember them as pressure-packed, an extremely uncertain time of life.

Different Doesn't Have to Be Bad

The common trap is to believe that if young people are so far removed in culture from their parents they must somehow be evil. This, of course, is not true. Teenagers are often the first to offer help to others, to be sensitive to the needs of younger siblings or older people. For every story of a teenage murderer or thief there is the counter-balance of heroism and kindness.

The temptations facing our youth today are simply more overt. More young people drink alcohol, use drugs, practice premarital sex, run away from home, commit suicide, and die from lifestyle choices than in any previous generation. The mere accessibility of so many abuses has greatly increased their chances of making wrong decisions.

When our daughter, Mary, was a student at the University of Nebraska, a newspaper account claimed that 98% of the student body drank alcohol. I asked her if she thought the numbers were accurate. She pondered for a moment and said, "I can't think who the 2% would be."

With the two major institutions of stability (home and school) pulled out from under many of them, teens today have lost their anchors in the storm of life.

The Pull to Grow Up Too Soon

It would be ideal if teenagers could take their time and adjust to life as it unfolds. Unfortunately, in today's world they are given little time to do this. They are often called on to make life-changing decisions as young as thirteen and fourteen.

They may be asked to

- have sex
- drink alcohol
- try drugs
- join a gang

Before they are old enough to drive a car they

are faced with addictive substances and practices against which they may not have the background and convictions to resist.

Add to these the more benign pressures of sports, girl/boy relationships, academic grades, and the search for independence, and you have an age group that faces more pressure than any other group in our society and the least amount of maturity by which to cope.

The school dropout rate is high partly because young people are torn apart. They are faced with a great deal of high expectations and less and less support to help them handle it.

Coming from a dysfunctional home, I was always amazed at the expectations of teachers and school administrators. They would say things like, "You'll have to get your parents to help you with this," or "Talk to your parents and see what they say." They pictured every home as a neat little package where the family offered plenty of support.

And how many more dysfunctional families are there today? The school supplies the pressure and expects the parents to pull the student through. But if the student can't count on his parents, the weight is heaped on his own shoulders. Too often teachers are insensitive to what they are asking from a shadow family.

Phantom Parents

There are a dozen reasons why parents are not available today. Some of the more frequent are

- divorce

- single parenthood
- careers
- multiple jobs
- recreation
- adult education
- travel
- social clubs

The missing or preoccupied parent adds considerably to the young person's dilemma. If no one is home, there is no one to talk to if he does feel like unloading his problems. And an empty house is an invitation to do what he might not do if there was an adult present.

Today's teenager can get condoms at school, drugs in the parking lot, a deadly sexually transmitted disease on the first date, beaten up for his jacket, addicted to alcohol at fifteen, an abortion at sixteen, and arrested as a minor for possession of drugs or alcohol.

They live in a different world, a new era, a time when more than ever the teenager needs a stable environment and all the help and support he can get.

12

How Well Do You Know Your Teen?

How well do you know and understand your own children? Before you throw that question out and say you know them pretty well, let's look a little closer.

First, what *should* you know about your teens, and then, exactly how much *do* you know about them?

Grab a piece of paper and answer the following questions by yourself. Then ask your teenager to answer the same questions.

Don't worry about failing. The goal is to increase your knowledge. When we gain knowledge we also improve our understanding.

Friends and Companions
1. Who are your teen's five closest friends?
2. Who is their best friend?

3. When did they last have a friend in your home?
4. What do they like to do with their friends?
5. Do they have a friend of the opposite sex? (How serious is that relationship?)
6. Has he or she lost a friend in the past year?

Activities
1. What do they like to do outside of school?
2. Where is your teenager at this hour?
3. If your teen was out past midnight, where would he likely be?
4. Does your teen like to participate in sports?
5. What electronic recreational gadget would he or she enjoy?

School
1. In a sentence, describe your teen's attitude toward school.
2. What is his or her favorite subject?
3. Who is his or her favorite teacher?
4. What were his or her grades on the last report card?
5. Does your teen want to go to college?
6. How much homework did he or she do last night?
7. What does your teen dislike the most about school?

Apprehensions and Fears
1. Name one thing your teen fears.
2. Name another thing your teen fears.
3. When your teen leaves home to take a major test at school, what is his or her emotional state?

4. Does your teen face real danger when he or she leaves the house? Explain.
5. Have there been armed youths at your teen's school?
6. Do gangs congregate at your local mall?

Parties

1. What does your teenager do when he or she goes to a party?
2. Would your teenager have a party at your house? Why or why not?
3. Are there adults present at the parties they attend?
4. Are parties special occasions, such as a birthday, or do the teens party simply to get together?

Dreams

1. What would your teen like to do after high school?
2. Where would he or she like to live?
3. Is your teen interested in college or a trade school?
4. Is your teen interested in marriage, career, both?

Temptation

1. Is there pressure on your teen to drink alcohol?
2. Has your teen ever been offered drugs?
3. Do you think your teen is under pressure to have sex?
4. Are there other major pressures that your teenager faces?

Only after you have recorded your own answers should these questions be taken to your teenager. Compare notes afterward to see how well you know and understand your child.

If this exchange does not seem too threatening to your teenager, perhaps he or she would like to talk about or discuss other subjects with you.

13

What the Teen Needs From Parents

Unfortunately, a teenager's actions will often be in contradiction with their feelings. They will complain, protest, rebel, and even threaten the parents they greatly admire.

A parent said, "I wish I had known what was going on with our oldest girl. I would have interacted differently with her."

Their daughter, Melissa, began to lash out against her parents while in her early teens. She threw fits, was rude and thoughtless, and insisted her parents were completely ignorant.

"I was sure she hated us," her mother explained. "And we had always been close. Instead of understanding the changes going on, we began to act like a couple of juveniles ourselves, which only made the problem worse."

Life will go smoother if we can accept three facts:

1. The teenager cares a great deal about his parents.
2. He is going through so much turmoil it is hard for him to express his true feelings.
3. A teenager will usually survive the period of conflict and move into a new and better relationship with his parents.

If your child were arrested in a foreign country, you would diligently attempt to seek his release, hoping that eventually you would prevail. Picture the teen years as a kind of temporary prison. Support your child, stand by him, help him in any way you can through the trials he faces, knowing that one day he will be released from this phase of his life. Secretly your teen is hoping that you will not give up on him.

The first thing a teenager would like his parents to know is that he loves them. He can't always verbalize it, and is frequently poor at showing it, but the fact remains.

Every Teenager Wants a Parent They Can Depend On

One of the worst things about living with a parent who has a problem with substance abuse is that the parent is not dependable. The child whose father tells her she can go out on a Friday night and takes away the privilege because he doesn't remember he gave it learns not to trust or depend on her father. And children who can't trust their fathers have a hard time trusting God or other authority figures.

A teenager, more than anyone, needs to know he can count on his parents to be honest, fair, and available. If a parent is consistently not around, the teen isn't going to feel that he can depend on that parent for help when he needs it. Often teens turn to other adults when parents are absent, and they may not be the adults you would want your teen to turn to. And if he finds no one else, he withdraws and trusts no one.

Trust is something that is learned and earned. Everyone needs a safe harbor where he can trust someone and be trusted. One of the greatest gifts we can give our young children is to let them know they can depend on us. This will then carry over into the teen years.

Dependability usually means a parent in residence. One girl told me, "Most of the time my dad is a phone call away. If the car breaks down, if I get hurt, if I flunk algebra, I know he will be close. He may not be able to change the situation, but he will be available."

Teenagers Need Adequate Praise

It's a basic human need. We all need reassurance that we are worthwhile people. Teenagers need an extra strong dose of it.

Remember, teens are going through a massive identity crisis. As adults, we at least have some vague idea of who we are and how we function best in this crazy world, but the teenager is at loose ends. Emotions are on a seesaw, mood swings are the norm, and the same questions keep flashing in their brains like neon signs: *Who am I? Does anyone love me? Who is God? Where do I fit in?*

Parents can help modify the teen's highs and lows with heavy doses of honest, appropriate, and timely praise.

It's hard to give our children something we never had. Many of us received little or no praise from our parents; consequently, we had poor role models to follow. That creates somewhat of a problem, but it is not insurmountable. Once we are aware of our weaknesses, we can begin to correct them.

An educator told me of his deep desire as a young man to become a minister. When he was nineteen, he spoke at a church near his home and his father attended the service. When they returned home afterward, the young man waited for some hint of approval from his father. Unfortunately, none came; his father never mentioned the event.

"If he had simply said, 'Not bad' or 'You have some potential,' I might be a minister today," the educator told me. "That's what I really wanted to be."

Appreciation for the Teen's Individuality

Early grade-school children tend to be extremely compliant. One of their main goals is to get their parents' approval. When they play cars they often imitate their parents' driving style, behavior, and attitude. They might select shoes or gloves to look grown-up, and grown-up usually means emulating their parents.

Those were golden years because everyone seemed to be moving in the same direction.

During the teen years the emphasis shifts. In their goal to reach their own identity, teenagers begin to break from the family pack. They want to declare their individuality. Normally that means they are changing groups. Instead of complying with their parents, they will now comply with their peers. Teenagers interpret this process as becoming an individual.

At this point the teenager needs a reasonable amount of freedom to seek that identity. A wise parent does not cut the rope, but lengthens it considerably, keeping a comfortable grip at one end. Parents need to broaden their concepts of music, dress, and personal preferences.

The art is in knowing how to control the slack in the rope. Part of a fisherman's skill is his feel of the line and how he responds to its motion. Parents have to slacken and tighten the line in response to the need.

Frequently they would like someone else to tell them how to maneuver the rope, but parents are the only ones who can judge what is right for their own child.

Creative Conflict and Confrontation

Teenagers expect reasonable conflict from their parents, and many realize that it is needed. They are not looking for drag-out fights, but neither do they want parents who are soft, letting them do whatever they want, without any concern for their well-being.

There is a time for testing the boundaries. Young people push and stretch them to see which ones are movable. A parent's role is to help the teen discover which are flexible and which are not.

A teenager needs and wants guidelines. But they also want parents who don't quibble over every detail. They want to be able to discuss with their parents things that are happening around them, like drinking, for instance. There shouldn't be any closed subject, if your teen wants to discuss it. The teen wants a confident parent who is not afraid to talk things over with them.

Of course there will be times when your teenager does not appreciate your guidelines and boundaries. Even if he knows they are reasonable, he may challenge them. This is not a sin on his part. He may be comparing your rules with those of his friends' parents, and you will need to give him some background and reasons behind your decisions. Keep in mind that some rules should be flexible, and even change with the teen's age and circumstances.

Your teens may even dislike you for a while, but don't take it personally. They might make fun of your clothes, your speech, your choice of recreation, your friends. But while they dislike you at times, they most likely love you.

Trying to discover where he fits in life is a traumatic experience. He tests all the possibilities. During this time of upheaval it is common for a teenager to dislike his parents and still respond positively to a survey on teens who love their parents.

Take most of their denunciations with a grain of salt. You are part of the world that they are temporarily at war with. Given time and experience they will eventually make peace with you. What they need now are solid, unshakable parents who refuse to let their teen's actions throw them permanently out of joint.

Teenagers Need to Fit Into the Family Like Other Members

A fifteen-year-old is not the center of the universe and neither is she the center of the family. Each member of a family is of equal value, parents and children included. When a family places its entire attention on a teenager, the youth receives more pressure than she can handle. Neglect is one extreme, but total focus of our energies on the teen becomes another problem.

By attending every single activity our children are involved in, we send a clear message: Our world stops for anything that happens in your life. The results can be less than positive.

1. The parents' relationship with each other degenerates for lack of other interests. These couples are at high risk to separate when the last child graduates.
2. Other children in the family are ignored, especially if they are not presently involved in many activities that the parents might attend.
3. Teenagers receive an exaggerated opinion of themselves if the world stops for them.
4. Some young people would like the relief of participating occasionally without the pressure of their parents in attendance.

Teens Need Parents Who Are Not Guilt-Ridden

We all know parents who feel guilty when their child fails. Every time her son Scott messed up, a woman we'll call Margaret went into a slump. She asked all the guilt questions. "What did I do wrong?" "Where did I fail?" "Was I too strict?" She thought she was a careless mother. She imagined that she needed to buy Scott more clothes, maybe even a car. She saw every problem Scott had as having its origin in herself. Margaret's self-incrimination made it difficult for Scott to own up to his own responsibilities.

Teenagers neither need nor respect a parent who is a scapegoat for them. If a parent continuously takes responsibility that belongs to the young person, that child as an adult may seek a marriage partner who will do the same. Don't shelter your teen from reality.

Teens Need Parents Who Are Financially Realistic

Parents who believe they can solve every problem with money create a shallow relationship with their teenagers. When a difficulty arises, they tend to buy something for the child as a quick solution. Of course it is usually not a solution at all. It is interesting to note that the parents who do this are not necessarily rich; in fact, they are often parents of meager means.

The temptation is to use money to improve status, to rescue from dilemmas, to show affection, to communicate, to erase guilt, to make up for an unhappy childhood. But by overspending, the time and work that a good relationship needs is often neglected, and a value system is developed that teaches the teen that money is the solution to all of life's difficulties.

A number of parents suggested that if they could raise their teenagers again, they would give them less money. Teens need the essentials of life, but giving them too much beyond that tends to produce ungrateful young people who see money as the basis of happiness.

Of course, there is no way to predict or guarantee how a young person will react to the provision of parents. Some will not allow too much to spoil him, and will be eager to make his own way. Others will demand more. Everyone must make their own moral choices at any age. And some will be grateful for a little or a lot, and actually be proud of a mother and father who hung in there with them through thick and thin. The Bible tells us, "Parents are the pride of their children" (Proverbs 17:6).

14

How to Argue With a Teenager

Can you picture the biblical Samson arguing with his parents? He saw an attractive Philistine girl and immediately knew he couldn't live without her. When he arrived home Samson told Mom and Dad that he had to marry this woman or he would simply die.

Shocked and perplexed, his parents argued heatedly that he could not marry a heathen girl. There were plenty of beautiful Jewish maidens, they insisted. Surely there was one who could catch Samson's fancy, bake bread, and keep the home fires burning.

Parents and son were equally adamant in their feelings. Each voiced their opinion and expressed their determination. When they were finally finished talking, Manoah, Samson's father, began to make the wedding arrangements.

Manoah could be the example of every parent who has ever argued toe to toe with his child—and lost. Most of us are not fond of arguing with our teenagers. It can be an ugly scene. Voices are raised; things are said that we wish we could retrieve; relationships become strained; and too frequently we end up losing the argument.

As distasteful as arguing is, the art of healthy discussion, even disagreement is vitally necessary. Parents and teens who never talk things over, never voice a disagreement, hold it all in and risk becoming bitter, resulting in no communication at all. The inability to discuss issues, even debate, makes us burrow into the ground and hide our feelings.

Teenage Lawyers

Listen in as a father and daughter debate over the Saturday night curfew.

"Be home by 12:00."
"Why?"
"Then I'll know you are safe."
"I'll be just as safe at 12:30."
"12:00 is plenty."
"Last weekend it was 12:30."
"You were at Sara's last weekend."
"So; I'm at Brenda's this weekend."
"Sara lives closer."
"Just ten minutes closer."
"Hey, be here."
"What if I call and tell you I'm okay?"
"You need to get up early Sunday."

"I promise to get up half an hour earlier Sunday."

"Then you'll be tired all day."

"I'll take a nap."

"You'll still be grouchy."

"Everyone else stays out later than I do."

"That's their business."

"They think I'm a baby."

"I don't care what they think."

"You don't understand me."

"I do too. I was a teenager once, you know."

"Things were different then. You had to milk cows."

"I did not."

"You walked two miles to school."

"Well, I did that."

"If you let me stay out later, I'll come in earlier next weekend."

"Well, okay. But just this once."

"Can I borrow five bucks?"

Teenagers can be quite clever and convincing when it comes to arguing a point. No longer in a mode to only please their parents, they are getting good at finding loopholes in their parents' logic. This is a major step in their separation ritual. They have begun to think on a similar plane as adults.

When they were younger and asked "Why?" the standard reply was "Because." They are too mentally sophisticated for that now. "Because I said so" needs a little more explanation, and you can count on the explanation being challenged.

Debating with a teenager can be exhausting. They are smart, quick, great observers, have terrific memories (when they want to remember), and they gather techniques from their friends and siblings. Young people come to court with a well-stocked arsenal.

On the other hand, parents often arrive empty-handed. They may even think an argument shouldn't happen because

- They think the teen should simply obey.
- They think there should be no negotiation.
- They are certain they know best.
- They refuse to be flexible as the youth grows older.
- They confuse the important with the peripheral.

Not all parents think this way, or are totally unprepared for confrontation. Some handle discussion or argument smoothly. But many of us learn the way it should have been done only after our teenagers have grown and left home.

Be firm when you need to be. If the situation should not be compromised, then don't compromise. Firmness at the right time provides security. Be willing to listen, but don't confuse the orange with the peel.

Let Your Teen Disagree

Lawyering is a basic need for teenagers. Be glad that they feel free to disagree and express it. The goal of parenting is not to say, "Our children agree with everything we say." If that's the case, then they have not yet blossomed to become themselves.

Spend some time debating your teenagers. We

show them respect by taking the time and energy to enter into discussion of the things that are important to them. Blowing them off without a hearing is demeaning.

One of the greatest gifts my high school English teacher gave me was when he would invite me over after school to talk with me about my writing. Each time he did it he bestowed dignity on me by saying in effect, "Your writing is worth discussing, even if I don't agree with everything about it."

There are three general areas that youth are most likely to question:

1. *Who says?*

This is the battle over authority. They dislike having their parents tell them what to do, and they absolutely hate anyone else telling them. Adults don't like being told what to do either, but they learn to allow for it. It is part of functioning as adults in our society.

My son used to say to me, "You're just trying to exercise your authority over me, aren't you?" He was very much attuned to his feelings—and sometimes to mine.

The authority issue makes it doubly difficult for stepparents. When a teenager is told what to do by a stepparent, he says to himself, *You aren't my father.* And sometimes he says it aloud.

However, it is crucial that young people understand that their parents are in a position of authority, and when necessary they will use that authority.

2. *How far can I push the line?*

If a parent says, "Be in early tonight," the teenager thinks, *How late can I be out and still call it early?* The parent may be thinking 10:00, and the teen is thinking 11:00. They want to see how far they can push it.

This is a question of boundaries. The parent sets them; the teen tests them. Parents need to decide ahead of time what the realistic boundaries will be, and then stick to them. Young people want boundaries, but their growing pains demand that they push them once in a while. In their heart they hope most of the boundaries will hold firm.

3. *How can I be free to be me?*

In no place is this more obvious than in the area of education. It is a continuous battleground because of the expectations of each. The teen wants to glide through school, doing average work. The parents badger him into excelling. If he gets C's or D's the parents are disappointed and show it.

Because parents often place worth, however unconsciously, on the basis of academic grades, the family is in a constant stage of conflict. Almost nightly, cries are heard throughout the house:

"Did you do your homework?"

"Yes, Mom."

"You better not flunk French."

"Do you think I'm dumb or something?"

"Why don't you bring books home?"

"I do!"

"You can forget borrowing the car until your work is done."

"Dad!"

In the midst of this, a teenager has three deep concerns:

- I'm glad you care enough to ask about school.

- If I get average grades or below, will you still love me?
- Why don't you let me take care of it myself?

Since school is such a major part of life and such an overwhelming concern for parents, arguments are bound to occur. These are born out of frustration and anger. Teenagers may be doing their best and still can't meet parents' expectations, or they may be working only to get by. That's why discussion is important. It can be a means of finding out at what level the teen is applying skills and for instilling the importance of education.

Smart parents encourage the interchange. They are not shocked by the impertinence of arguing, but rather they keep their cool and help their teenager work it out.

13 Tips for Arguing With Teenagers

1. Pick your place—a quiet atmosphere, preferably.
2. Choose your battles carefully. Don't argue for the sake of arguing.
3. Keep to the subject. Don't bring up past failures of two years ago.
4. Never degrade the teenager; simply seek to correct a wrong behavior.
5. Be firm but not rigid. If their idea is right and good, accept it as such.
6. *Never* get physical. This does not help discussion, and will certainly harm the ego.
7. Be completely honest. Anything less will destroy trust.
8. Don't overload the discussion with too many

subjects. Keep to the point.

9. Set a time limit, and continue the discussion later when you've reached it.

10. Negotiate. Be flexible. Accept their suggestions when they are valid.

11. Admit you are wrong, if you are.

12. Compliment, but don't flatter. Point out their real strengths.

13. Pray for a good attitude before and during your discussion.

Remember, not everything is negotiable, but most things are debatable. If a teenager challenges a parent's decisions, that's wholesome. Be steadfast over what is vital, but still be willing to discuss the matter.

15

Bribes and Rewards

When we first became parents, I thought the idea of giving a child an award for good behavior was preposterous. Who ever concocted the notion that children should receive something just for being good? I can only speak for myself, but I believe that God converted my way of thinking. By His grace I soon learned how important rewards are for children.

Rewards are vital for everyone, in fact. A few years ago we talked to a thousand people about their marriages and found that payback is essential to a happy relationship. Spouses who didn't feel compensated for their efforts tended to sabotage their relationship. They felt sorry for themselves and backed off.

Our friends in business and industry say the same thing. A paycheck isn't enough. Incentive pay, educational programs, softball teams, special recognition, and other perks are all part of rewarding good work.

Even the Bible speaks of rewards. "Watch out that you do not lose what you have worked for, but that you may be rewarded fully" (2 John 8). "The man who plants and the man who waters have one purpose, and each will be rewarded according to his own labor" (1 Corinthians 3:8).

Rewarding Teens

If the concept of rewards for good behavior works well for others, why not use it for teenagers? If that sounds frightening to you, it was for me too at first. We would like to think that good conduct is its own reward, but that isn't always true.

Teenagers, almost more than anyone, need positive reinforcement. When they put in extra effort they like to know that someone notices and cares.

At one point my wife, Pat, and I discovered that we had taken so many privileges away from our teenagers that if they got into trouble again there wouldn't be any privileges left to take away.

It isn't hard to identify the adults whose parents were stingy with rewards. Those adults seldom compliment anyone; their speech is highly negative. They specialize in finding fault, and find it difficult to offer encouragement. Their role models were stern and punitive. For most of us, it is extremely difficult to rise above our role models. The good news is that the grace of God can help us rise above them and exercise a generous spirit.

Rewards, Not Bribes

Those who have the most trouble with the idea of giving rewards may be confusing rewards with bribes. If you promise to pay your teenager for good behavior, that's a bribe, and it's the wrong approach. But if you reinforce good behavior with a reward after the fact, it can be a great motivator.

If your teenager shows responsibility when using the family car, offer it to him when least expected. Volunteer to send him to a camp of his choosing if he shows promise in a sport, for instance. If he reaches out to some new kids at school, offer to provide videos and pizza at your house, so he can invite his new friends over.

If you only offer to pay for something that you would like the teenager to have or do for your own prestige or satisfaction, you are manipulating. Most teens grow up to resent that type of bribery.

A daily goal should be to catch your teenager doing something good. It's a welcome emphasis. And when you do catch them in the act of good behavior be sure to reward them.

How Many Rewards?

In his excellent book *The Family,* Dr. Paul Welter discusses the reward-punishment ratio.[1] He suggests that we take stock of how often we encourage family members and how frequently we discourage them. Welter says he has seen parent/child relationships that run as high as 1 to 20 in favor of the negative.

Try to imagine an atmosphere where encouragement is that rare. Yet some teenagers live in homes where rewards are nonexistent.

Any raising of that ratio toward the positive is

[1]Dr. Paul Welter, *The Family* (Wheaton, Ill.: Tyndale House Publishers, Inc., 1982), p. 228.

a step in the right direction for the healthy, well-rounded nurturing of a teenager. Many will have to work hard to increase the level, but the benefits will amaze you.

Of course there is the possibility that a parent could overdo the giving of rewards and demoralize the young person. I don't think too many of us are in danger of that, however.

What Are the Good Rewards?

Trips to Mexico or skiing in the Alps make coveted rewards, but they aren't really necessary. The rewards or prizes that really matter are far simpler, and cheaper. Let's look at a few.

1. *Body Language*

When we interact with our teens, what does our body language say? Is our face screwed up? Does our brow furrow? Do we make fists without thinking, or sit cross-legged with our arms folded tightly against our chest?

Open, relaxed body language can be a gift. It tells our children that we are not locking them out. Our warm, empathetic expression says they are welcomed and loved. A hug or a hand on their shoulder won't cost a dime.

2. *Voice and Tone*

Too many of us have developed a permanent whine. We are constantly complaining about our teenagers' conduct and performance.

A cheerful voice, an approving tone will help them relax and become less defensive. As parents, we are responsible for setting the mood in our families, controlling the atmosphere in the home.

What we say and how we say it goes a long way in setting the tone for rational conversation and comfortable dialogue. Give the gifts of encouragement and a positive attitude.

3. *Events and Recreation*

Keep the privileges coming their way. You aren't buying them off when you furnish them with some enjoyment and entertainment.

Create memorable experiences like fishing, bowling, traveling, sports games, shopping, crafts, or any other event that teenagers will go along with. Don't push them into doing these things, but find out what they enjoy and either provide the opportunity for them and their friends or make it a family outing. These are the benefits of a solid relationship.

4. *Immediate Rewards*

Thirteen-year-olds have trouble tying into college as a reward. That's why it is often ineffective to tell a youth that he will need his good grades six years from now. The prospect of a trip six months away has limited effect. Teenagers generally have short-term goals. Reinforcement that comes this weekend or this month is of greater value to him.

Try to keep your teenager from developing an attitude of "What's the use? Nothing works out anyway." That type of thinking is devastating. Keep on top of what's happening in his life and provide positive reinforcement consistently and often.

16

Kidnapped by Their Peers

Third and fourth graders tend to admire their parents. They go on trips together, spend Saturday afternoons fixing the lawnmower, go fishing, or bake cookies. Parents make children feel safe and loved and they like to be around them.

Parents are a child's key to the world. They unlock mysteries and introduce new adventures. For parents who are in residence and available these are years of closeness and satisfaction.

Then, one day, the parents notice that their child is missing. The boy or girl who used to be so near and so dependent seems to be around less and less.

It's almost as if the child has been kidnapped. He's turned thirteen and his new friends or peers have stolen him away and introduced him to another world. That new world has opportunities, experiences, and places to explore that parents could never provide.

Bonding with peers when you are a teenager is like being kidnapped because you are forced to go whether you want to or not. Children leave the safe harbor of their childhood and test the seas with others their own age.

The average young teen is excited and fearful at the prospect. Growing up, making decisions, discovering a new level with friends, trying new lifestyles, all sound fascinating. But they also know they can get hurt in the new world. They go with their captors complete with a broad smile and a pounding heart.

What Peers Have to Offer

Friends are more than a luxury. As surely as they need iron in their blood, teenagers need peers to help stabilize them as they grow. Contemporaries are essential to their sense of wholeness and balance.

What are they getting from these friends?

- acceptance (inclusion)
- rejection (exclusion)
- personal identity
- group identity
- faithfulness
- betrayal
- superficiality
- honesty
- confidence
- love (different from family)

- sexual attraction
- self-worth
- compromise
- forgiveness
- companionship

Children are limited in their mobility, their choices, their maturity. They collect most of their experiences and values from their parents and siblings. Teenagers learn to give and take in a greater way and there is much more at stake.

One phenomenon teenagers face early on is social strata. Some of them described to me their frustrations. They found it nearly impossible to date across social lines. Teens from lower-income homes, for example, don't ask teens from upper-level income families out on a date. It simply isn't done. Parents frown on it; their friends look down on it; their social backgrounds reject it.

Many lessons or social norms that are learned by teenagers will stand them in good stead all their lives. And some may even make breakthroughs and headway that we never dreamed possible in our day.

Going to Extremes

With so many adjustments to make, few young people are able to keep it all in balance all of the time. They may work too hard for acceptance or take rejection too seriously. Unable to fit into one group they may choose friends who are troublesome. Anxious for love and acceptance they may try alcohol or drugs or sexual experience.

This age group from the beginning of time has

groped with the transitional period of adolescence to adulthood. But with each era it seems to become more complicated. Today's teenagers grapple with a greater mix of diverse value systems and questionable moralities, and they are less likely to receive the majority of influences from extended family members.

Teenagers today are highly mobile and have a great deal of financial freedom. They are introduced to a wide choice of lifestyles, probably more than they can handle at their age.

The writer of Proverbs was well acquainted with the problem of selecting friends or companions. Even in that day, with limited exposure, parents worried about their children and their friends.

"He who walks with the wise grows wise, but a companion of fools suffers harm" (13:20).

"Do not envy wicked men, do not desire their company; for their hearts plot violence, and their lips talk about making trouble" (24:1).

The teen most likely to go to extremes is the one who suffers a poor self-image. Girls who are sexually promiscuous are usually struggling to make friends. As contemptible as the behavior is, your heart goes out to them. The respect and acceptance they so desperately want is denied.

Fortunately most teenagers go to less extremes, but they may allow their new friends to change their value systems in exchange for acceptance. In some cases they may steal or lie or defy authority simply to better their standing with their peers. Unable to approve of themselves, they are frantic in their search for approval by their companions.

Two-thirds of teenagers are unhappy with themselves, and are thus highly prone to need peer approval. Every day thousands of teenagers do something they really don't want to do, whether it be drinking, smoking, taking drugs, or having sex. But they feel trapped, as if they have no choice. They don't want to be left out. They don't want to be rejected. They are willing to pay a high price for acceptance. The pain of being alone or isolated is too great.

The real prize of life is not to have a host of friends, but to have a few valuable, dependable, steady ones. We must teach our young people that and hope that they come to the same conclusion.

"A man of many companions may come to ruin, but there is a friend who sticks closer than a brother" (Proverbs 18:24).

Peer Isn't a Four-Letter Word

Don't panic at the thought of your child having peers. Friends are also capable of good influence. Many a parent has sat back in their favorite chair and breathed a sigh of relief when their teenager walks out the door with a happy, wholesome companion.

When our daughter, Mary, was a teenager, she and a group of her friends were eating at a local fast-food place. As they finished their meal, the waitress came over to their table and told them their food had been paid for. The woman sitting in the next booth was so impressed with their wholesome behavior that she paid for their meals and slipped out quietly. Talk about rewards!

They were a good group all right. They didn't need to drink, smoke, swear, or swing from the chandeliers to have a good time.

Whenever possible, provide a setting where your teenagers and their friends can meet, and where they can meet others of like faith or value systems. The church, youth group, Christian camp, your home, all are excellent places. Don't force it, but provide gentle encouragement.

If your teen brings home a friend that you can see is a positive influence for him or her, make that person feel especially welcome and hope the friendship lasts a long time.

Peers Are Small Groups

You could compare the support groups that many adults attend to the peer groups your teens involve themselves with. Many benefits and special bonding are found in small groups. Those feelings are similar to what teenagers experience with their friends. They are validated and empowered by relating one on one with others their own age, with similar problems and dreams.

If someone criticized the small group you were a part of, you would probably be offended and become defensive. You would feel hurt and likely draw closer to the members of the group. That gives you an idea why teenagers react strongly if we knock their friends. Those friends are very important to their self-esteem and growth as an individual.

What About Questionable Friends?

It happens too often. Your daughter shows up with a new friend. The girl is wearing a motorcycle jacket, has a tattoo on her left hand that says "Party all night," and her breath smells like an ashtray.

What's a parent to do? How do you warn your daughter without sending her into a tantrum and losing her forever? Here are a few tips:

1. *Stay calm.* Don't say something you'll regret later.
2. *Be humble.* Your daughter may think this girl is great, or maybe she is trying to reach out to her. Don't make her choose between her friend and her parents.
3. *Express your concerns.* Privately, of course. Don't touch on the superficial, such as criticizing the girl's hairstyle or dress. Explain the one or two real problems you have with this person. Don't exaggerate. Give your daughter something to think about without bringing it up every waking hour.
4. *Invite the friend in.* If the new girl seems to be a regular with your daughter, ask your daughter to bring her into your home. The last thing you need is a hostile relationship with your teenager's peers. Besides, an accepting, caring adult may be just what the friend needs.
5. *Offer alternatives.* Support every level-headed Christian youth activity within a hundred miles. Make them available to your teenagers, but don't push.
6. *Pray constantly.* Pray for yourself. Ask God to make you loving, fair, and firm. We can't control others, but God will help us get a handle on ourselves. Pray for your child. And pray for your child's friends.

We can't choose our children's friends. We can

only guide them in their choice by setting a good example and teaching them good values. Then we hope and pray that they will see which friends are really the best for them. Be supportive every chance you get.

17

Counseling Your Teenagers

You may be sitting in the living room late at night reading a magazine, when suddenly you notice something move ever so slightly to your left. You look up to see your teenage daughter has quietly planted herself on the couch. Staring at her shoes she mumbles a barely audible, "Hi."

Considering the communication you two have had lately, your daughter is taking a big chance. She needs someone who will listen to her, someone to try a few ideas on, maybe even give her a little counseling. She doesn't normally go to her parents to discuss her personal problems, but she would like to try.

You're both a little nervous at this point, wondering who will speak first, how to connect. Does she really want to reach out this time? Do you have anything to say to her? Will it lead to misunderstanding and more tension?

This is not an unusual scenario. Most parents and their teenaged children will come together in a similar setting at some time or other. It may be after a date, or before a date; when they are considering going to a drinking party or other questionable function; after an argument with a friend; while considering a serious spiritual decision; or even when thinking about a career.

When a teenager has successfully cleared the hurdles and actually approaches a parent for counseling, whether he thinks of it as that or not, will the parent be prepared? in any way be of help? Believe it or not, teenagers would like to make a positive connection with an adult from time to time.

It is true that some parents and their teens relate in an easy fashion, and enter into conversations that involve counseling on a regular basis. But these relationships are rare.

There are certain guidelines or keys that make it more likely that your teen will seek you out and that the counseling given will prove helpful.

Fourteen Keys for Parent-Counselors

1. *Work on relationship.* If there is friction or a great distance between you, the opportunity for counsel is less likely. Parental counseling begins in the family room playing board games, shooting pool, or watching television together. Work hard on getting to know your teens and liking them.

2. *Maintain open settings.* Biking, hiking, traveling; or shopping, baking, conversing in the kitchen, provide some of the best opportunities for counseling your teens. Talking to your son while

watching football together is less threatening than pulling the son into a closed room and saying, "We've got to talk." Teenagers don't like to feel trapped.

3. *Be available.* As we mentioned before, you can create an atmosphere for talking with your teens just by how you act around them and your tone of voice when you speak to them. Lighten up. Maintain your sense of humor. Remain calm and relaxed. Being available might mean some late hours. For some reason, teens like to talk between midnight and 2:00 A.M. Have the coffee ready and be patient.

4. *Be an active listener.* Three-fourths of the time a teen needs someone to listen. Don't talk too much or control the conversation. Contribute comments aimed at stimulating the conversation, but first and foremost be a listener.

5. *Respect their privacy.* Usually what your teen shares with you is spoken in confidence, even if it doesn't seem confidential to you. You may ask, "Is it all right if I tell your father?" If the answer is no, keep it to yourself. Obviously, it will not be information to tell the neighbors, relatives, or their friends' parents. Keep it between you and your child unless he or she specifies otherwise.

6. *Keep advice to a minimum.* If you are asked advice on a subject, suggest a couple of options. Allow your teen to make his own choices. Don't decide everything for him. If there seems to be only one choice in a matter, ask him if he can think of others.

7. *Raise questions.* Open-ended, and sometimes direct questions help the teen to think something through. Stay clear of questions that can be

answered with a simple yes or no. These tend to shut down the flow of conversation.

8. *Stay calm.* If your daughter says she wants to be a bartender when she is of age, don't hyperventilate. Keep your cool and say, "Why does this career appeal to you?" She may be trying to shock you to see how you will respond, or there may be some underlying problem she is trying to deal with.

9. *Share experiences.* My daughter asked me how long I dated her mother before I knew I wanted to marry her. I gave a short answer and turned the conversation back to her. It was a question that deserved an honest answer, even though I may not have wanted her to base a current decision on what I did. Teens need to see that you are human, that you went through what they are going through and you survived. Share your experiences, but don't turn it into a history of your life.

10. *Don't take her choices personally.* If a daughter is thinking about dating a drummer in a rock band, don't take that as a rejection of your values. If you act hurt, you cut off your chances for being objective. Concentrate on her decision-making process. You can get counseling later for your bruised ego.

11. *Hold on the judgment.* Instant judgment is one of the biggest obstacles to parent-counseling. If a daughter says bluntly, "Last week I had sex with Kevin," what are you likely to say or do in response? Will you condemn her verbally and send her to her room, condemn him and accuse him of rape, call his parents, ground your daughter forever, or preach at her about the sin of fornication? Try looking her in the eye and saying calmly, "Was

that something you wanted to do? How do you feel about it now?" You have just opened the way for further conversation and counsel.

12. *Negotiate.* Whenever possible, make suggestions as to how you might or might not be able to help in a given situation. Keep an open mind to solutions that you might not have considered before. Guide them in solving problems themselves.

13. *Suggest options.* Options are extremely important. Suggest several, even if some of them are not likely to be used. Having limited courses to pursue can be devastating to a teenager. When they feel they have no place to turn, they tend to do nothing, or give up.

14. *Tell them you'll pray.* It may not be convenient or appropriate to pray at that moment, but assure them that you do and will pray for them. They need to be reminded of the power of God and assured of His working in the situation. They aren't alone in facing the problem.

How many times have you quoted a piece of wisdom that you picked up from your parents? Do you catch yourself repeating an axiom about marriage or racism or finances that you remember your mother or father saying? The influence of parents on teenagers is greater than you might think. That influence can be even more constructive if parents improve their counseling skills. You don't need a formal degree to increase your availability or your skill in conversation and counseling when your teenager seeks it.

All of us have gained wisdom from our own life experiences. Surely we would like to pass a fair amount of that wisdom on to the children we love. The trick is to find the right openings and pass the wisdom along carefully. Like a relay team passing a baton, it must be done at the correct time and handed off in a sure-handed manner.

> My son, pay attention to my wisdom,
> listen well to my words of insight,
> that you may maintain discretion
> and your lips may preserve knowledge.
> (Proverbs 5:1)

18

Trouble With the Truth

"I can't work with a kid who will lie to me." The mother who said this was trying to block out her teenager's behavior, but at the same time was blocking him out. Lying was such a horrendous breach of trust to her that she couldn't deal with the other problems.

Most parents are shocked and perplexed when they discover that their teen is loose with the truth. They would far rather wrestle with broken curfews, shattered promises, failing grades, back-talk, or even drinking, than be directly lied to. It's almost as if the moral vase has been cracked and can never be mended.

In a perfect world no one would tell a lie. We are not in a perfect world, and our teenagers are not perfect. They will occasionally resort to a heavy distortion of the facts.

Why does a teen select this route? How should a parent react? Let's lay the facts out.

Why Does a Teenager Lie?

They are afraid of what the truth will do. The truth can be painful and have adverse consequences in the short run. If they say they haven't completed their homework they won't be able to go out. A "little" lie will allow them to go to the party; the truth may get them grounded.

Their attitude is adult-like. Given a certain set of circumstances many (if not most) adults would lie. While we are shocked that our children would lie to us, they are not so different from most parents. Anyone who has lied on his income-tax return, told half-truths in notes sent to school, or distorted the facts in applying for a credit card should not be shocked that his teen lies to him.

They are under incredible pressure. Under more stress than they think they can handle, teens often feel the need to lie. If everyone's going to a party, they can't tell their friends (a) I'm going to stay home and do homework, (b) My parents have grounded me, (c) My mother needs me at home. In our dreams we may wish they would say that, but the odds aren't good.

They aren't sure they can trust their parents. If a parent responds unreasonably when his teen tells him something, the teenager begins to think his parent can't handle the truth. Then he blames the parent for the fact that he is spoon-feeding him half-truths, white lies, and outright whoppers.

It becomes a game. Some teens learn to enjoy the art of lying. Their attitude is, "They can't prove anything anyway." These young people lie even when there is no pressure to do so, and deception becomes a joke. They are in for real trouble later on.

What's a Parent to Do?

When a parent knows his teenager is lying, he needs to confront him. God gave parents the responsibility of establishing and reinforcing moral boundaries. Teens need a clear set of values, no gray areas.

But before you rush to your teenager and confront him with his error, there are some admonitions to keep in mind.

Know the facts. A lot of damage is done by false accusation. Children are in a tough position. They are not expected to defend themselves or "talk back." Too many parents think they "just know" when they don't.

Be humble. The minute we swing into a tirade about lying, the teenager may be saying to himself, *I remember when you lied.* And he could be perfectly correct. Try to see his perspective.

Be clear on the fact that lying is wrong. The Bible doesn't mince words about lying (see Colossians 3:9). Teenagers may be confused about the matter. They don't know many people who don't manipulate the truth.

Don't take a lie personally. When someone says, "He lied to me," I usually hear an emphasis on the last two words. We are insulted and hurt. In order to be of help, though, we have to get over the personal pain. Deal with the larger issue.

Remember your own adolescence. Did you never lie to your parents? Did you never go someplace and tell your parents you didn't? Keep your feet on the ground. Most teenagers are very much like ourselves.

We all wanted perfect children. That wasn't

possible—look at their parents. We must first accept teenagers as they are—imperfect, and yet love them anyway before we can get anywhere with teaching them anything.

19

The Need to Believe

Teenagers don't have to be told they are sinners. Drowning in guilt and insecurity, most know instinctively that they have a black hole the size of Pittsburgh. If anything, they are carrying too much shame around.

In an uptight, hectic, pressure-packed, temptation-ridden, evil world, they would like to find someone who understands their problems and is strong enough to help. Not every teenager is ready or willing to meet Christ, but many would be responsive if someone explained to them how the Son of God connects with their needs.

Aaron became a Christian at the age of fifteen. Later he explained what drew him to faith. The three things with which he identified were

- acceptance
- forgiveness
- purpose

When someone told him these were available

in Christ, God became personal to him, and he was ready to believe. These are the areas in which a young person feels the most deficient. He feels inadequate and rejected by the adult world. With all the change going on in his body and surroundings, he is continuously unsettled. He may wonder what the point of living is if each day is only filled with upheaval and uncertainty.

Simply telling a teen he should go to church is seldom effective. It sounds like supporting a cause. It comes across as an admonition to act responsibly; do the right thing. You owe it to God to be in His building. If there is some validity in that approach, young people are unlikely to identify with it.

Adults today may be ministered to by a well-ordered service complete with standard hymns and organ music. Teenagers are very unlikely to identify with that kind of worship. There is a vast culture gap between adult religious expression and that of a teenager.

Actually, they are more likely to dedicate themselves to a personal God who loves and accepts them than they are to an institution. They more easily develop a sense of allegiance to a group of caring believers than some adults do. If a young person feels understood, helped, and welcomed, he will lock onto that group.

Teenagers are quick to see the difference between religious routine and true spirituality. They don't play religious games. (That usually comes with adulthood.)

An Unsteady Faith

Because life doesn't always follow a straight, smooth line in other areas, when a teenager becomes a believer he may walk a rocky road of faith at first. He has difficulty focusing on one project for very long, and will likely have trouble with personal discipline in the realm of spiritual things as well.

It is easy for adults to interpret a teen's fickleness as a lack of serious dedication. Today he does or says something that suggests a mature faith; tomorrow the principal calls, and he's in trouble. What kind of faith is it? It's young faith. Like the experience of the apostle Peter, the sincerity of faith cannot always be measured by behavior.

I became a Christian while in high school and within a year I was president of the Bible Club. What I lacked in wisdom I more than made up for in enthusiasm. We had regular meetings, brought in speakers, led in prayer at assemblies, and generally made our presence known on campus.

While we were up-front about our faith, we also managed to be normal teenagers. We skipped classes, got sent to the principal's office, and engaged in outrageous pranks.

Eventually, we were confronted by the principal about the apparent inconsistency. He wondered why our participation in the Bible Club didn't produce in us better behavior. To which I replied, "I don't know."

Today, the answer seems obvious. Our deportment did not always match our profession of faith because (1) we were human, and (2) we were teenagers. Human behavior is not always consistent, and a teenager's faith does not necessarily influence every area of his life.

My pastor also had trouble with our uneven lifestyle. He seemed to think I should behave like a teenaged deacon.

Maturity must precede mature spirituality. When a young person becomes a Christian, he does not cease to be a teenager. The most spiritually minded young people can become involved in the most bizarre behavior.

To paraphrase Paul's passage in 1 Corinthians 13:11:

"When I was a teenager, I talked like a teenager, I thought like a teenager, I reasoned like a teenager. When I became a man, I put a teenager's ways behind me."

Don't discount a teenager's faith because he doesn't act like a saint.

True Spirituality

We often confuse spirituality with form and practice. We encourage young people to read the Bible regularly, pray before meals, attend church services, and listen to Christian radio. This may be all well and good, but it doesn't necessarily produce spiritually minded young people.

Many youth are wise beyond their years and know better. They don't buy religious routine for spirituality. While they may not know *how* to become spiritual, they recognize the product when they see it. They see parents and other adults as spiritual who live in a loving, caring, tolerant, patient, forgiving, and accepting manner. They know that a parent who practices all the religious routines on Sunday, but lives like an ogre at home, is not spiritual.

Who Joins Cults?

Teenagers who are frustrated in their search for genuine faith will often turn to cults. This is es-

pecially true when two elements have character-
ized their background. (1) They suffered rigid le-
galism in the home and were not allowed to find
God in their own way. Rules and regulations were
at the heart of all that was taught. (2) They received
little or no personal attention in the church or religious circle they, or their family, were a part of.
"Keep the faith" was all that was important.

When that individual finds a group that cares
for him and meets his needs, he often joins it no
matter how extreme its doctrines or beliefs might
be. The young person can even deal with the le-
galism that might exist in the cult because of the
caring structure and real fellowship that go along
with it.

The Teen's Battle With the Church

Most parents will eventually have to deal with
the question of whether or not to force their teenagers to attend church. It's a tough and agonizing
decision. Someday your teenager will look you in
the eye and say, "I am not going to church."

What is the correct response?

Many parents will not give their teenager a
choice in the matter. They will say something like,
"You'll go to church as long as you live in this
house," or some other authoritarian statement. In
some cases where this tactic is used, those young
people will conform and turn out to be great leaders in the church or the community, and be none
the worse for having simply obeyed their parents'
mandate.

It is not wrong to insist on family cooperation
in such matters. However, that unbending position

doesn't always work for everyone. Some teens can hardly wait to get away from home and make their own choices. And when they do, they often do exactly the opposite of what they were taught in the home.

One alternative response might be to say, "I know you feel uncomfortable in our church. How about taking the fourth Sunday of each month and attending the church of your choice?" Sometimes just the freedom to choose is all that is wanting.

You may even want to go so far as to say that when your teen is a senior in high school she may decide when she goes to church. Don't say, "You are free to skip church." Rather, make it a choice as to when she attends.

There is no perfect response. If I knew of one I would give it here. But there is more than one way to deal with the issue, and each parent must find what works best for their family.

It is a known fact that many college students and other young adults who are away from home have chosen to avoid church attendance. They are trying to break from their childhood in that area too. Parents could make the transition easier by loosening the reins earlier, even in the matter of religious training.

Spiritual Transition

Expect your teenagers to challenge your personal faith and practices. It is an important step toward making their own spiritual commitment. It does not mean they are evil or godless. They may be simply looking for a faith in Christ that they can call their own.

Here are some things parents can do to help:

1. Keep your own spirituality fresh, strong, and warm.
2. Be supportive of a youth group that meets the spiritual and cultural needs of teenagers.
3. Within the guidelines of Christianity, allow your teens to differentiate themselves from your religious practices.
4. Let your teenagers see your faith lived out daily in practical ways.

During their younger years, it was easier to tell your children what to believe in and how to practice it. Somewhere in the teen years those children will have to make their own personal decisions about what they believe in and how they express it. When they marry and have families of their own, they may seek the more structured setting for their own children. But they must be given some freedom during the teen years so that they find it easier to make good choices when they are adults and on their own.

20

The Need for Forgiveness

If ever there was a slate that needed to be wiped clean, it is the one on which is written the things said and done during the adolescent years; the things that have caused untold damage to both parents and children. Everyone makes mistakes, but we are talking about those words and actions that have never been forgiven and forgotten. If bitterness sets in and we carry grudges against our teenagers, we run the risk of marring our relationship with them for the rest of our lives.

One wise person said it this way: "We can either hold on to the grudge and lose the person, or hold on to the person and lose the grudge."

The choice is before us. Unfortunately, many parents allow self-pity to shackle them into resentment. Their teenager has hurt them deeply, and that hurt has turned into anger. Anger over a period of time degenerates into bitterness that can eat at the soul for a lifetime.

"He took money out of my wallet!" one dad complained. "I didn't raise my kid to be a thief. I gave him plenty of money, and he turned around and stole from me. Can you imagine it?"

There is no doubt what the boy did was wrong. He should have been corrected and disciplined at the time. There is also reason for the parent to have felt hurt, betrayed. But ten years later? The parent must forgive his son and concentrate on nurturing the relationship. While it may sound simple, many parents find it extremely difficult to let go of their resentment.

We Can't Revise History

Some of us would like to turn the pages back and have someone tell us that it didn't really happen. We want to have it explained away. Or we want our son to tell us what made him do such a thing. If he would just explain why, we might understand that he really isn't a thief. We want an apology at least. If he says he's sorry, then we might be able to let the bitter memory out of the iron box.

Consequently we deal with two improbabilities: We may never understand why he did what he did; and he is not likely to throw himself at our feet and beg forgiveness.

A young lady dropped out of college after two years to pursue a career in music. Her parents were disappointed that she didn't get her B.A. degree in education. Years later, they have agreed not to talk about it but remain hurt.

What do these parents want from their daughter? Do they want her to say she secretly got her degree through night school and they've worried over nothing? Do they want her to admit that they were right and she should have continued in teacher's college? Or do they want her to realize her mistake and beg them to help her finish her degree now? What would it take for them to rid themselves of stored up bitterness and resentment?

The Extent of the Hurt

There is no doubt that teenagers hurt their parents. It is bound to happen during such a stressful transition period in their lives. Usually the teen is not aware that he is hurting his parents, and if he is, he may be sorry but doesn't know how to deal with it and stop hurting them. Forgiveness is something that must be offered even when there is no confession or repentance on the part of the offender.

The fact is, we are largely responsible for how much we hurt and how long we nurse that hurt. If my teenager lied to me today, I would feel terribly hurt. He would be wrong; the fault would lie with him. If, however, I felt the same pain two months from now, I would be the one who is acting unreasonably. The teenager gave me the pain, but I decided to carry it and keep it fresh.

There are parents who have reminded themselves daily for ten years that their teenager stole from them. The teenager gave the burden; they decided to carry it.

The issue will never be resolved, and the pain will never be eased unless we are willing to forgive the child who has hurt us. If we are out to get even and settle every score, we will sacrifice the relationship.

We can be insulted, betrayed, ignored, but the extent of the damage done by the hurt depends on us. If someone puts a hot coal in your hand it will burn the flesh. But how long you hold the coal is up to you. If you have any sense, you won't hold it for long.

We Will Never Be Pain-Free

Part of the price of caring and loving is to experience some pain. The goal isn't to become pain-free. That would be unrealistic.

If you have a son in prison, a daughter on drugs, a grown child married to an abusive spouse, you would be less than human to say you had no pain. The sense of loss alone will cause untold grief. What we have been addressing is the pain that has turned to bitterness because we refuse to forgive.

The Fear of Forgiveness

When sixteen-year-old Tanya became pregnant, her entire family went into shock and turmoil. There were raised voices and accusations. Many ugly things were said that family members may have regretted but did nothing to erase them. Those scenes were burned into their memories.

Five years later, everyone is on speaking terms, but if you are around them you can feel the tension. Tanya's father doesn't talk about the matter, hasn't said much about it for years. Her mother helps take care of Tanya's child while Tanya attends a trade school.

Each person in the family performs his or her role in the drama and carries the hurt just below the surface. *If only this hadn't happened,* they reason, their lives would have been so much better.

Regardless of adjustments they have made, none of them has really forgiven Tanya, and she hasn't forgiven her family for how they treated her when she needed their support the most. Each feels betrayed, guilty, and resentful. Why can't they forgive?

There are several dynamics that come into play in a situation like this, but none more significant than the fact that everyone is *afraid* to forgive. They have established a relationship centered on guilt and blame. It is difficult and painful, but familiar, almost comfortable. If they step out now, five years later, and forgive, they will be venturing into new, uncharted territory. That would involve a lot of risk, because they have forgotten how to forgive, accept, and love one another unconditionally. And if someone does say they are sorry, they may fear they will not be forgiven.

As amazing as it may seem we can become accustomed to a sick relationship. In the family just described, Tanya's pregnancy defined the members. In other families it may be the stolen money, the stolen car, the alcohol problem, dropping out of school. Each of these hurts has been allowed to control the way family members respond to one another. No one wants to lay it aside and begin again.

Forgiveness is at the heart of Christianity. The Lord has forgiven us, and this should enable us to forgive others. From the Sermon on the Mount through the Pauline Epistles the message is the same. When we refuse to forgive, we limit what Jesus Christ can accomplish in our lives.

Accepting the Teenager, Imperfections and All

None of us expects our children to be perfect, or do we? When our child messes up, we are hurt by the shattered dream. What went wrong? What did we do wrong?

We are crushed by the broken promise, the betrayal of trust, the blow to our pride. "I knew he wasn't perfect, but why did he have to do *that*?"

Maybe in our heart of hearts we actually thought our kid might turn out to be perfect. Now the dream is destroyed and we have trouble accepting our teenager, imperfections and all.

The child of our flesh, raised in a Christian home, taught moral values and decency, has let us down. It still comes down to the fact that we must let go of the personal hurt and be willing to forgive and get on with what is truly important: loving the teenager for who he is, in spite of what he may have done.

Conclusion

There Is Reason to Hope!

On Christmas morning our family sat around the kitchen table eating breakfast, waiting to open presents. All three of our children are in their twenties now; all beyond the tumultuous teens. But as I sat there, my mind wandered back to those days. I thought about the braces, the dates, the conflicts, the laughs, the spiritual battles, the trips and family outings. I could still picture them helping our neighbor, wearing grungy jeans, going to concerts, acting in school plays, and the inevitable confrontations, jaw to jaw.

I smiled to myself. The bad times weren't worth thinking about. There was too much love and forgiveness and hope in the room that day to dwell on any disappointments we may have experienced. We talked about a myriad of subjects: politics, football, faith, love, boyfriends, marriage, and relatives. We played Ping-Pong, worked puzzles, and ate everything in sight.

Each of us has a lot of great memories, but that isn't where we live. Families can't live on memories alone. Smart families keep today alive and drink it to its fullest.

Parents and their teenagers have much reason to hope. After you have walked together through some pretty heavy times, you will emerge one day as happy, grateful people who appreciate one another even more because you have gone through some difficulties.

You will discover that there simply aren't answers to everything. Magic formulas that work for one family do not work for another. There are no ABC's of raising teenagers.

It's all right *not* to have all the answers. Nobody does. When you've set the best example you can, your job is to love your teenager, support him, and forgive him. The rewards come when they are grown.

People to Thank. . . .

I can't remember all the people who helped with this book, let alone thank them. Groups and individual adults and teenagers all over the country gave of themselves, and I am grateful to them. Special accolades go to my wife, Pat, for her work, encouragement, and love. I also want to thank our children for taking us through the teen years laughing, learning, and crying.

There is one group of teens who deserve extra recognition. They came more than once to our living room, ate pizza, and told us what it is like to be a teenager.

Thanks to:

Jana Breese	Aaron Oswald
Charlie Janzen	Vicki Smith
Kristi Ketchum	Chris Widga

May every teenager have attitudes as good as theirs.